CHUB AND DACE

CHUB & DACE

John Bailey & Roger Miller

The Crowood Press

First published in 1990 by
The Crowood Press
Ramsbury, Marlborough
Wiltshire SN8 2HE

British Library Cataloguing in Publication Data

Bailey, John
Chub and dace.
1. Chub. Angling.   2. Dace. Angling
I. Title   II. Miller, Roger, *1958–*
799.1752

ISBN 1 85223 243 9

Typeset by Inforum Typesetting, Portsmouth
Printed in Great Britain by Redwood Press Ltd,
Melksham, Wilts

Contents

Acknowledgements

We would both like to express our sincere thanks and appreciation to the following gentlemen who have, to the man, made such invaluable contributions to this work. Not all are writers, but all have shaped this book whether they know it or not! They are: Frank Barlow, Archie Braddock, Brian Bush, Martin James, Dicky Kefford, John Gower, Tony Miles, Roger Nudd, Alan Rawden, 'Reelscreamer', Pete Rogers, Christopher Shortis, Peter Smith, Neil Stewart, Fred Sykes, Chris Turnbull and finally, Trefor West.

Introduction

The inspiration for this book is comparatively simple: for a long while the Wye river and many of its tributaries built up a growing, although misty, reputation for holding very large chub indeed. It was during the summer of 1985 that I talked to Chris Yates at a meeting on the Royalty stretch of the Hampshire Avon; he told me of uniquely large chub reported from the middle and upper beats of the Wye. The precise locations were, frustratingly, not known by Chris – or certainly not given away that evening – but he was sure that record breakers actually existed there. This was enough for me, and the following summer saw me tour that valley for a long period, actually meeting a man who claimed a near-6lb chub from the region of the

Many of the Wye's tributaries built up a growing although misty reputation for holding very large chub indeed.

Black Mountains. Valuable information was gradually accumulated in that first visit, but it was not until the autumn of 1987 that the inimitable Roger Miller and I spent some time on the middle reaches, albeit for barbel, and to a lesser degree pike, with the result that we hammered the chub population to fish well over 5lb. The river there, salmon water *par excellence*, seemed a chubber's paradise, with dozens of pristine chub being caught. All were very hard-fighting, unmarked fish and, although 5lb 5oz was the best taken, the chances of something significantly greater seemed ever-present, so every time we struck at the jerking quivertip, our hearts were in our mouths.

The story resumes in the Christmas period of 1988 when I returned to the river, to a beat further upstream. The weather was astonishingly mild; daytime temperatures were in the low 50s Fahrenheit. There was virtually no wind and, day after day, light values were very low. It really did seem that the quest for a very large chub was to be blessed with success. From the first, many generally small chub came out. Chub to just over 3lb fell to every conceivable method, even floating crust, from a river system that ran low and clear, containing a lot of fresh, green weed. The fishing was nothing less than fun (which is vital), and spectacular (which is excellent), but the big ones were frustratingly slow to arrive. After four days I spoke with Peter Smith, a good friend and our host at the hotel. Peter, a notorious veteran of the English carping scene, knows more than possibly anyone else about all the species of the Wye system. He pondered on the problem for hours, for the whole evening almost, until at last he spoke. 'There are only a few places at the moment that I'd recommend for a genuinely big chub, I mean a *really* big chub. You know, the sort of chub you see swimming free when you're stalking, and later on when lying in the bath you think, "Good grief, it couldn't have been that big . . . could it?" '

He held his hands out wide in front of him and continued, 'The Wye is too large by far to really get to grips with in the winter, in the limited time you've got. They're still in there, certainly, but you can't see them easily like you can in summer. No, it's best to stick with the tributaries, and my hunch would be the little stretch at X. It's small and intimate, not full of chub perhaps, but the mammoth chub are there. It's an easy river to read too – as though Crabtree had been along marking all the chub swims with his capital 'Xs'. The level will be good. The big fish are there. The weather is brilliant and holding. If you're a half-decent chub man all you need to do is get out there and just do it!'

Needless to say, very early the following morning found me and a trusty companion in the drizzle-laden mist of some obscure Welsh valley which little knew what season of the year was upon it. There had been no frost. There was no dew, just the rain from the branches quite willing, if not yet ready, to shoot. There were, though, the grim reminders that the winter cycle was on its course: here and there on the beaches of the river lay dead salmon kelts. They were tragic, spawned-out specimens, failing in their hopeless return to the very distant sea. The stillness of the air only intensified the stench of the last, dead salmon. In the gloom the carcasses looked pathetic – their skulls bleeding, their eyes crying at the low water – and the draping cloud refused to flood and wash their bodies to the decency of a salt-water tomb.

My companion, not a deeply involved angler, found the valley moodily oppressive and intimidating in a heavy, baleful fashion. I was too involved with the river itself to appreciate the atmosphere around me fully. It was exactly as Peter had described it. It was lavishly tree-clad and wound through steep, wooded hillsides. In every way, it was a chubber's paradise. I put my gear down at the head of the beat and simply drooled. Walking a hundred yards or so, I came to the most enticing of rafts and then moved on to see an energetic ripple emptying into a slow, deep pool. From there on down, the river was a never-ending succession of deep, eddying runs beneath overhanging alders, long glides, mini weirs and, in fact, just about everything that made for a dawn of indecision.

I began by feeding bread into four of the prime swims, after checking along the bankside for signs of recent anglers. There was no indication whatsoever on the mud, the sand or the lush vegetation. The only tracks of a hunter were those of a heron which had probably been stalking the margin's tiddlers. There was no litter but that which lay feet up the bank, high and dry, and left by a long-forgotten spate. The thrill that grips the angler on a near-virgin coarse fishery was taking hold.

The swim under the raft on the far bank was surprisingly rapid and, despite a good deal of weight, the bait trundled through far too fast for my liking. Worse still was the shallowness of the swim. At only two feet deep I felt little confidence in it, and moved on. Slightly beneath me my companion took a decent fish from under the roots of an alder, a hard-fighting and pretty little chub of about 2lb 12oz, perfect in every way. However, this was not, obviously, the calibre of fish our mission was about.

Together we moved to the streamy water at the head of a slow, eddying pool. We sat there for quite a while, feeding in more bread, taking in the soft greys of the valley around us. Eventually I cast, and the large lump of flake rolled enticingly through the currents, barely hampered by the single SSG shot a foot above it. Through my fingers I felt the river suck the bait, engulf it and swish it even further from me. But rivers do not nip! They do not draw with such power and urgency! I struck, and within fifteen seconds I knew I was connected with a chub the likes of which I had never felt before. The single, solid rush of a hooked chub a man is ready for, but not this never-ending drive downstream to escape. For a full three minutes the fish bored further and further away. Salmon? Barbel? A chub foulhooked? All these options ran through my mind, and with a spool low of line I decided to clamp down on the fish, bring it to the top and get perhaps an inkling of what the dawn was about. The strain was quite terrible but the tide, it seemed, had turned and the bull had been seized by the nose. Two further minutes — a lifetime — saw line back on the spool, and ten yards below me I saw a chub as it turned its head again to the sea. Under pressure the fish rose in the water. I saw its tail, then its back and finally a head with line direct to the top lip!

The hook pulled free!

I still refuse to say how big I thought that chub to be, but the fire was rekindled within me. As I sat on that wet Welsh sandbank the loss of that great fish ran through me with a flood of grief. I remembered back a dozen years to the River Yare in East Anglia when, roaming, I'd hooked my first

The scene of John Bailey's despair — the lost Wye Goliath.

monster chub on a size 18 hook and gossamer line. That fish had also fought on and on, leading me a hundred or more yards before it, too, inevitably broke free. The pain then had been hard to bear, but it was not as scorching as this new loss. From that moment the drive for chub, especially these Welsh chub, was suddenly born within me; I determined to capture a massive one . . . or at least give everything in the attempt.

I was well aware of Miller's love/hate relationship with the species, which in reality was hate only when a 3lb nuisance fish charged around his pre-baited roach swim! I knew that his early days on the border river, the Waveney, had bred a passion for chub as strong as mine. Reading his Waveney Tale below, it is easy to see why.

The Waveney river, God bless her, was on reflection, I suppose, well on its way to its present-day ruin when I expected so much from her. Local villages like the historic Hoxne, the lesser-known Needham and that ancient big-roach domain Sylham, were all names that were quite simply so synonymous with wonderful river fishing that nobody ever assumed that they would ever be anything else. These stretches are synonymous today, sadly, with pig slurry pollution and crazy de-watering foul-ups. I have realised that in my teens I caught the old river 'twixt the two extremes.

The very visible, introduced chub compensated the anglers.

Introduction

While the big, indigenous roach verged on extinction the very visible, introduced chub compensated the anglers, as they have done for years, as the true essence of the Norfolk and Suffolk rivers died around them. All this was of course way over my head then, and my early memories of the Waveney are of a lightly fished, prolific chub fishing mecca. At that time, the famous old carp catcher of Redmire fame, Dicky Kefford, lived in a beautiful old miller's cottage right in the middle of the focal point of my chub fishing world, and though he will probably not be able to remember the impressionable but rather precocious youth that was his pupil, I shall never forget his quiet words of encouragement when things went wrong. One particualr day stands out from a memorable summer holiday; let me tell you of it.

The only word to describe those summer holiday bicycle rides to the Waveney valley is probably 'expedition'. A caravan of transport would be pedalled from the village, through two more, before we enjoyed a whole day on the river – Dicky probably dreaded our arrival. Gradually our numbers decreased, with the faithful few falling into established routines; Kevin hunting out loach and bullheads beneath the stones, Andrew and Timothy mesmerised by the dace shoals, and Rodney always spinning for jack.

The chub, we had decided, were totally uncatchable – they would lie beneath a weeping willow in a mini weir-pool, a shoal of six, visible from the tree and apparently impregnable. They were my passion then, and old Dicky knew it. Regarded by the others as a bit of a crank for setting my heart on them, I resolved to catch one, or die trying.

I think what I found so exciting about those six chub was the fact that one could observe them for hours at a time. Their pleasant lifestyles could be witnessed amid the lush, waving 'cabbages', the pure water and the spotlessly clean gravel; imagination was unnecessary. Their seemingly aimless drifting around the eddy, occasionally sipping in something or other from the surface film, their periodic chasing each other with the sun glinting on their flanks was real, not a scene lifted from my angling books that I had come to know so well. I lived for no other world than theirs.

The old carp catcher suggested crust, floating on the surface, left to drift around above them until one of them could resist no longer. With the huge square of crust dunked and then cast, I followed his advice. A method dimly recalled from an old carp book, it nevertheless appeared exciting and new to me. Suddenly, from beneath the willow that unforgettable bow-wave emerged; like a torpedo it surged towards the drifting crust before a huge, white slurping mouth engulfed the crust with a violent splash. Mesmerised,

I shall never forget that almost black pig of a fish glinting in that summer holiday sunshine.

I watched the line tighten. The strike was pure reaction and the chub was on! I whooped in my excitement – the wood-pigeons flapped madly from the chestnuts, the dog began to bark, and Dicky offered gentle words of advice as panic ensued around him. Back towards the willows the fish bored, but I followed Dicky's advice and soon it was in the tiny landing net.

I shall never forget that almost-black pig of a fish glinting in the summer holiday sunshine as the rest of the gang suddenly appeared from all corners. Although all of them have drifted away from my life and angling now, I know that that old chub left its mark on each of them for a very long time indeed.

The rusty old salters registered '3lb 12oz', and Dicky was as pleased as I. I was a hero now, and how I loved it! That chub and the way I had caught it left such an impression on me that I considered no other species, or method, for years.

So it was that February 1989 found Miller and I back in the Wye valley with helpers, bait and all the willpower we possessed. A monster chub – perhaps

Miller and Bailey's helpers not yet aware of the 'keeping below the sky line' rule.

the lost Goliath – was a voiced objective but we both knew how high the chances were against our finding it. We were also there to enjoy the great river and its tributaries for the chubbing paradise it so surely was. It is doubtful, to the best of our knowledge, if any other British river system has so much to offer. There are all types of water to discover and fish; there are the rushing rapids, the massive pools, the huge runs of the main river and all the intimate twists and turns of the smaller, less awesome, tributaries. For mile upon mile chub swims that have never even seen coarse anglers abound, whole beats that have only known the salmon angler's fly or spoon; there are scores of miles of untapped potential with such variety of swim type that every skill and method in the chub angler's repertoire can be called upon. Peter, the hotelier, would be our mentor; fate would decide if our combined enthusiasm would prove sufficient to conquer the giants of the Wye!

The Night Fishing Approach

John Bailey

The weather seemed to be mild once more. The period of bright, sunny weather had blown away somewhere over England and the east, and by midday Friday, the next depression of the month was plodding its weary way down the great Welsh valley. As it approached, the temperature began to rise again, the colours faded from the scene and the sky blackened to bring drizzle and, occasionally, harder rain. All in all, this was the obvious night to try the Great Hotel Bend.

There were two things that attracted me to this deep, mysterious stretch of water, some 100 yards long, running sluggishly beneath cliffs and precipice, overhung with sweeping trees. First and foremost, Peter had spoken of a

A nocturnal chub from 'The Great Hotel Bend'.

15

5lb 15oz and a 6lb 2oz chub which had been taken from the pool in recent times. I felt that this was probably a repeat capture of a single, excellent fish. It indicated that the chub was a resident of the pool and very likely still to be at home there. She could possibly be even larger than the last recorded weights, as the spawning season approached. Whatever, I felt the chances of a six-pound chub were enticingly real; something I had long wanted now seemed very possible.

Secondly, I felt some confidence in the swim because initially it appeared a very typical chub hole, much like ones I had experienced in the past. Why? It simply did *not* fish by day; Peter said as much. A blank session during my previous visit confirmed his experience. If the job on the Hotel Bend were to be done at all successfully, then it was a night affair or nothing . . . and nothing gives me greater pleasure than a night affair!

Peter had recommended a bait of bread mash earlier in the day, and I had carried this out religiously. I took half a bucket of well-soaked bread, with treats of cheese and lobworms included. A dash of cheese essence, which I felt would do no harm at all, was also mixed into the sloppy concoction. I felt the half-bucket of bait would be enough to interest the chub, yet would be nowhere near enough to feed them up – after all, I had once witnessed a single 3lb chub eat a whole pound of cheese and six slices of bread on its own. As I put out the bait, the whole pool appeared dead and quite without life. I watched the food drift untouched through the slow, deep, clear water. The little that floated was carried away unattacked on the current. To all intents and purposes, the pool was quite chubless. But experience told me otherwise; there are some places that fish *only* at night.

Late afternoon, and preparation was a half-light-hearted and a half-serious affair. Miller had fished very hard all day for some decent chub, and had returned to the hotel too tired for the night bash. It must be added that fatigue did not prevent him trying to pour port down us, paint dire pictures of the coming weather and generally attempt to sabotage the entire enterprise. For my companion and I, the affair was more serious. The Great Hotel Bend is very long, which would give both of us the chance to fish. My companion would be lower down in the easier paced water, whilst I would be on the deeper, swifter, snaggier area. We both had our targets – mine the 'six-pounder', and hers the first 'four' – and that placing on the Hotel Bend seemed the most likely for both of us to stand a chance. The sense of possible achievement was therefore with us both and we talked almost in whispers, even up there by the hotel, a quarter of a mile from the swim.

The check on the gear was completed . . . and repeated. The rods were ready, assembled with 4lb line straight through and with the exact lead we

A nocturnal chub of 5lb 2oz which proves the value of fishing into darkness.

knew we would need in place. My companion put on 3 SSG to hold bottom whilst I used 2 SSG to allow the bait a slow trundle past rock holes, tree stumps or the hide of any big fish. What else? . . . two cushions, two rod rests, two landing nets, and bread, cheese and lobs in plenty. She took a torch but I would not risk one in this clear water. And, after all, I had 30-odd extra years of experience of controlling tackle and of feeling the line behave between my fingers. What we did have were two hopeful hearts, and off we went. Our footsteps crunched past the bar where glasses were raised to us by the Millers in now-genuine good wishes, past the last of the lights and off into the heart of the darkness. We had to cross a swing bridge, which was no easy task in the dusk, when the rain had polished the moss on the ancient planks to ice and glass. Safely across, we were on the far bank track, moving along the left of the river to the Great Hotel Bend where we settled as noiselessly as possible fifty or sixty yards apart.

The light closed down even further and the mildness increased, if anything. As the wind died utterly away the drizzle became more a wet, cloying mist over us. Little by little my companion's torch beam took on an even bolder profile through the night, and the salmon left in the pool enjoyed a period of leaping. Poor souls. They were stale, tired fish, still fruitlessly hoping to arrive at the long-deserted spawning redds, yet fated to suffer a lingering death in their futile drift back to the sea. Their splashing echoed hollowly off the cliffs opposite like mocking laughter. Owls called constantly up and down the well-wooded valley, and if my companion's torch shifted its angle, the beams disturbed the roost of pheasants in the trees facing us.

For a good while, the pool seemed as dead as it was during the day. We sat through a period of complete inactivity, despite feeding in more bread and constantly changing the bait size and its placing. As they will, the worries began to creep in. Had the pool been netted or emptied of fish by devilish cyanide poachers? Had our approach over the stones to the water's edge been too noisy? Was my companion's torchlight scaring fish in the low, clear water? Was bread, however flavoured, a blown bait? Had too much flavouring been introduced and driven the fish downriver? Or was it simply one of those nights when the best-laid of plans goes inexplicably astray?

Then I heard my companion's rod whistle in the damp air. She had struck - unsuccessfully, she whispered – at a sharp knock. Perhaps it was a dace –

Alan Rawden and some Norfolk night life.

like the ones that seemed to be tugging and twitching at my own line now. In the slack at my feet a few small fish scattered. Dace again? Or small trout? But what was frightening them? The minutes crept on and, as they did so, the slight indications on my line ceased as though smaller fish had left – or been forced from – the scene. My expectancy was real. At times I held my breath; I felt my heartbeat right to my hands and the blood pulse in my fingers only a skin's depth beneath the lightly held line. Across and downstream of me, a fish wallowed heavily. Surely chub were on the move.

It was now two hours after dark and the earlier warmth was fast dispersing. The mist was no longer a blanket but a shroud, cold, penetrating and unpleasant. I found myself beginning to look at my watch, wondering if my companion had had enough, when her rod struck through the night a second time. Now, though, I saw it stop and bend over against the glow of the widely diffused torch beam. Even the sound of the rod action had been different: a satisfying 'thwack' rather than the empty whistle of failure. Her fish was fighting hard and deep like all the Wye system chub do. Night lent drama to the occasion, and when the fish finally splashed it was with eerie suddenness. Soon the angle between line and rod decreased and I searched the water before us with the beam. A foot below, a twenty-inch bar of silver reflected back the light in a glow of dazzling beauty and power. And then she cradled it . . . 3lb of exceptionally lovely chub.

From here on, our night became hectic. Between us we accounted for seven fish, all alike as podded peas, and without a hint of the fabled 'six' or even the yearned-for 'four'. Each time the line tingled, grew tight and pulled decisively into my flesh, each time my rod lifted in a vibrant energy I felt a thrill of hope that dissolved in the first ten yards of the fish's run. The sensation I awaited – a movement of immovable heaviness followed by a run of irrepressible power – did not occur. My big chub had moved on. Or had it learned to avoid bread? Or had the gyrations of its struggling comrades rung the alarm? Perhaps the fish had turned total predator. Could it be that the biggest of the chub was waiting for the night to draw on even more before emerging from its cavern under the slate cliff? Could the fish even be dead? Optimistically, I hung on and on, and yet sometimes I feared that the 'six' had been nothing but legend from the start.

Eventually, our concentration fortunately snapped at precisely the same time. I lost a typical fish through a moment's absent-mindedness and six inches of slack line. My companion dropped a fish as she admired it – only six inches, quite harmlessly on to a bed of soft sacking – but it was enough. We packed in seconds and within minutes were by the bar, in the way every winter chub night session must ideally end. Warmth at last. In a glow of

A 5lb 11oz nocturnal chub proves the theory.

fellowship and satisfaction, we basked in the lessons learned and fired the rest of the night with plans anew.

For both Miller and I, our faith in chub night fishing is rooted in Wensum experience. John Wilson's work of the 1970s is important. Diving Hellesdon mill-pool just north of Norwich, he found the chub during the day stacked into an undercut bank. He had discovered their desire for shelter and their avoidance of light and he went on to develop the argument in his chapter on chub in the book *The Big Fish Scene* (edited by Frank Guttfield: Ernest Benn, 1978). John wrote about how fish hide during the day and come out of snags as the light decreases.

Everything he said then was confirmed by our own experience of roach fishing. At night, roach captures were interspersed with the occasional very large chub that almost never showed during daylight hours. When I moved to a mill house on the Wensum very close to Norwich, my eyes were further opened. The river there was, and still is, very, very heavily fished and even then the chub were awake to all the anglers' tricks. Almost all the chub have been caught before and the continual bankside disturbance makes them wary and unsettled. Their tendency as a result is to seek sanctuary under branches, rafts, undercut banks (a favourite) or in thick weed.

Big chub seek sanctuary under branches.

Massive baiting with corn, hemp or maggots will draw them from cover and they will begin to feed avidly, but they are clever, streetwise dudes of chub that will rarely take a hookbait. After darkness, however, the angler is at last in with a chance. Suspicions are lowered and the chub will begin to pick up hookbaits, but even then it is strictly necessary to keep to fairly light tackle. I believe chub on all rivers have a preference for nocturnal feeding and this, I know, is intensified by heavy angling pressure.

In winter during cold weather, whenever there is slow, clear water, this tendency is only increased. During the 1986–87 season I fished hard for those Wensum dudes and found I could only get at them a long time after dark. The worse the weather, the further on into the night I had to wait. Warmer or flood conditions did bring forward the spell a little, but as soon as the weather changed it was at once a late night business again. Once the chub began to feed, my experience suggested that they would carry on for three to four hours before bites began to taper off and the swim grew quiet again. Disturbance could have been the cause of this, but more likely I believe it to be the nature of the chub itself.

The Lost Day

Roger Miller

The breakfast was a sumptuous affair of massively ornate pots of Earl Grey tea, and hot croissants steaming beside kippers as large as haddock. Mine host, Peter, joined us and, as always, had us in a lather as to what we should do that day. The choice eventually came down to two – mine and that of the rest of the party! And so it was that my trio of companions dropped me by the tiny Normandy church that for 900 years had overlooked a coil of silver, etched through sheep-dotted downs of green and brown hues and shades. That minor tributary of the Wye was represented on the map by the thinnest of blue lines and was perhaps, Peter had at last confided, where the largest of all Wye chub could be found – he had seen such a specimen there with his own eyes.

The mile-and-a-half stretch of river, coveted by salmon men in the summer, and by this pursuer of chub in the winter, was available in exchange for a £1 coin at the village shop. Such was the astonishment as he incredulously uttered the word, 'Chub?' that I simply cowered in my humiliation.

'Back at four!' the funsters had cried as they left me to walk that mile-and-a-half of river alone, and there was hardly a yard where I thought a chub was unlikely to be. At the bottom limit of the beat a sudden rock scree barred any further investigation as it cast sinister shadows over deep, sombre water of gentle swirls and creamy foam coming from the upstream rapids.

I found myself unaccountably anxious, fraught and unsettled. However, immersed in my own thoughts I climbed to the top of a nearby hillock and pondered my reaction. The absolute greyness that had now descended, that beautiful 'soft' weather that is essentially Irish (but at times Welsh) obscured the view. It obscured the church and the lane along which my friends had departed, it obscured the whole world, and suddenly the stream and I were quite alone. I gazed upon the eerie scene and gradually my thoughts focused. Here lay a stream of such perfection that I could see before me, reproduced as if by watercolour, every chub swim I had ever loved elsewhere.

A coil of silver etched through sheep-dotted downs.

My whole chub fishing career lay before me. As my eye followed the stretch it was like turning the pages of a scrap-book, with each swim and kindred memories flooding back. I have no idea how long I sat up there but every success and failure was relived; my time was spent with these memories, and these memories became the only place I would cast that day.

'THE BUSHES'

During the winter of 1976/77, whilst walking round the massive 'New Pit' at Weybread during a Pike Anglers' Club Fish-In, I suddenly found myself chatting to a strangely familiar piker who eventually introduced himself as Barrie Rickards. If ever a day was to change my life then this was most definitely the one!

Introduced by Barrie over lunch to a couple of the Norwich crowd I was soon conversing at length to one who is now an old friend, that marvellous photographer and taxidermist Neil Stewart, about the only species I really knew anything about at that time – chub. He was a Wensum man; I knew nothing of the Wensum, and he nothing of the Waveney. My favourite stretch skirted the pit, and as the pike were slow I showed him round.

Neil was enthusiastic about the Waveney, and so it was that we shared a rod and simply roamed. I had not cast a bait for three years, the desire having left me in those late teenage years, and although I did not realise it at the time, the old feeling was returning. Why else was I haunting my old domains, nosing round, studying glides and rafts, enjoying the smell of water and the sound of the river? For the first time in years I felt the satisfaction of a freelined bait, in this case a big old black slug that used to litter the meadows, plopping into the undercut bank where I had caught so many chub as a schoolboy. Fate certainly took a hand that day as the slack of the line suddenly zipped tight and a chub was on. It was as if I had never been away.

At 4lb 1oz it was my biggest ever, by far! Neil said it was a promising start, and slipped it back. I was stunned! 'Not even a photograph, old chap?' I whined pitifully.

'It's only a low four, why bother?' came the reply. It was the biggest chub I had ever seen! Neil suddenly realised what he had done; the Waveney was certainly not the Wensum, and he felt guilty at his nonchalance. This was the moment at which I first heard of the thing that has caused me more ecstasy, heartbreak, passion, sadness and obsession that anything I have ever known – that loveliest of rivers, the Wensum.

It was as if I had never been away.

There was a syndicate, Neil said; two miles of chub infested river, write to the farmer, mention my name – and keep your fingers crossed. The reply came a few days later – positive, I was in. And there began the greatest chub fishing I have ever known.

The Thursday after I had met Neil for the first time at Weybread was the night of the monthly Pike Anglers' Club meeting in Norwich. I decided to take the afternoon off work and spend it walking the stretch I had just joined, perhaps having a go at dusk if I found a swim I fancied. With only a rough map supplied by the farmer I eventually stood before a river that was wider, deeper, clearer, faster, richer and much lovelier than the one I was used to nearer home. I walked, and walked, and walked that afternoon before at last managing to get my enthusiasm in check and settle on a swim.

There were so many to choose from! My eventual choice was to be a familiar one to me over the succeeding months, but on my first visit to it I simply drooled. A thick, virtually impenetrable spinny of tangled alder, hawthorn and stunted oak stood before me, and a very mature alder had fallen across the river creating the biggest raft I had ever seen. Three-quarters of the river was covered with a vast area of debris gathered over time, and it looked the most mouth-watering swim I had ever seen.

*I was convinced that scores of chub lived beneath the cloak
of security so beloved of these fish.*

The racy current was deflected by the raft, and it was a simple matter of
casting to the lip of the raft and letting the current push the lightly shotted
line beneath the cloak of security so beloved of chub. I was convinced that
scores of chub lived beneath that raft. I later learned that they did not,
which was always a great mystery to me; but the giant roach more than
made up for the chubs' absence. However, giant roach are a tale not
destined for these pages!

The neon glow of Norwich was now visible downstream as darkness
seeped into the grey light of the afternoon, and rolling mists swirled their
way towards the city. With my world now almost totally stained by the
blackness I realised I was softened by three years of warm, cosy, comfort-
able places of hedonism, far away from the wilds of the East Anglian
floodplains! I huddled ever-deeper into woollen jumpers as my feet tingled
with cold. I wondered how I managed to stay away from such glorious
anticipation for so long. The bait, which I distinctly recall as soft cheese
paste, was suddenly and dramatically taken, the betalite smacked against
the rod butt, but the cruel emptiness of a missed strike was all I could feel as
I responded as firmly as I could. With my heart racing I took three attempts
to place the bait where I needed to for it to end up deep within the raft. In the

now total darkness I sat quietly as the bobbin settled down, flicking occasionally as a leaf or something brushed the line.

Five o'clock came, then six, eventually seven; my trap as yet unsprung, I began considering packing up and attending the meeting. I was simply excited at just being there. Seven-thirty was the cut-off point, but somewhere between the two saw the bobbin flick twice. My frozen hand hovered above the rod in nerve-jangling anticipation, the bobbin jerked then transformed itself into a green blur before cracking against the butt for the second time that evening.

The chub was on, and how that chub's initial rush impressed me. Upstream and downstream it powered itself; netted, gasping and beaten it lay before me, as to my considerable angst I realised I had no damn torch! I could feel that the fish was huge, far bigger than my four-pounder taken on the previous Sunday – never had I know such frustration. I knew I had caught a giant amongst chub, if only I could see it. In wild excitement I ran the mile (no comments please Mr Bailey) to the car, drove to a telephone box and dialled Neil. Mother says he's left for the meeting; phone the meeting, no, he's not there yet, can he phone you when he arrives, I should say! He phones. With camera and torch he arrives, and we race down the floodplain. How long it is, it's never-ending, I tell him. I cannot even weigh the thing let alone see it.

An hour had passed since the fish took the bait and at last I was gazing down upon it. I had been right, it was an exceptionally long fish, but quite thin too. 'Good grief' was all Neil could say, apart from '5lb 3oz' and 'Well done'. What outrageous good fortune! But the Wensum, I was to find, always makes you pay for your successes with a lot of failures. However, that night was one of the rare ones and I was greeted as a hero upon my eventual arrival at the meeting. It was at that moment that my love of angling for better fish really took off. Friends made that night are still friends today, and it was the events of that evening which made me fully realise that I had found exactly what I was looking for. I returned to the swim several times after that, but I never caught another chub there again. Indeed everybody who knew the stretch said it was a poor chub swim. After a while rapists in the guise of Anglian Water Authority employees ripped out the obstruction and the raft disappeared forever, taking the big roach with it. I was also to learn that no county in England has such a capacity for self-destruction as Norfolk has, by those 'in charge'.

Alan Rawden with a 'Long Run' fish of 5lb 4oz taken on the tip.

THE LONG RUN

A stretch of the Wensum that I knew well had the appearance of a layer of bends resembling an inner intestine, U-bends of great depth with alders darkening the water, and you could always be sure that I would settle there and ignore the long, poker-straight, featureless, canal-like 100 yards that followed it. Beds of rushes, like the floating reed islands of Lake Titicaca in Peru, prevented anything but a moorhen from reaching the river and sinking without trace.

Stupidly, I had chosen to ignore this run and whilst I had fished the top bends for months, with moderate success, the sanctuary of the 'Long Run' was not apparent to me. Yet it was obvious! The whole stretch was well fished, with most of the conventional chub-holding features regularly seeing baits and producing fish to the faithful. Apart from its virtual impenetrability, the other major factor that prevented the Long Run from seeing either angler or bait was, I think, that it simply looked so barren of features, and therefore of chub. Wrong!

It looked so barren.

I recall vividly one July day swimming some floating crust through the top bends with about one in every five crusts being engulfed by the chub. Obviously a lot of free samples of crust were finding their way into the Long Run, with a steady stream of bait tempting anything that was there. Ensconced as I was amidst the cool shade of the alders it was the sound of those violent, vicious and so carefree takes that initially grabbed my attention. There was an area of high ground on the inside of the last bend that afforded a panoramic vista of the scene. The Long Run, which I had written off together with everybody else, was, I was astonished to see, a mass of swirling, bow-waving, crust-slurping chub! And what chub! Not fish in the usual 3 to 4lb class, but fish of far greater size, with one or two breath-taking specimens. The whole scene resembled trout madness during a mayfly hatch on the upper Bure. At that moment I realised many things, not least that the sanctuary of chub that lay before me were eminently catchable and unknown to all.

I needed no other prompting, and the first crust I allowed to drift through this stewpond-like scene was perhaps the most dramatically taken bait of the whole day. A bow-wave from the opposite bank ripped its way across

It disappeared leaving a pattern of ever-decreasing circles.

At 4lb 4oz, it was a very exciting introduction to the 'Long Run' chub.

the stream for a distance of at least ten yards, seemingly hell-bent on that massive fragment of farmhouse white. As it disappeared amidst a flurry of spray the gently uncoiling line accelerated its pace and drew tight. My strike was probably unnecessary but I hit it firmly, and at 50 yards the chub took off in a burst of enthusiasm equal to that of its approach to the bait. At 4lb 4oz it was a very exciting introduction to the Long Run chub.

The boost those Long Run chub gave to my confidence and enthusiasm was phenomenal really I suppose, and it was the way in which I was forced to develop my floating crust technique during that summer which I associate with the Long Run most of all.

When that memorable day was at last finished, as the sun sunk like a flaming ship behind Ringland Hills, I thought I had the method and the Long Run totally sorted out, but in the words of old J.B. – the more I knew, the less I knew! This was certainly the case as I returned again and again to that same run. What follows is how my approach was developed over the succeeding weeks, in order to keep one step ahead of the larger than average chub I found the Long Run to contain . . .

That first day saw chub smashing into crust as if there was no tomorrow, and without rhyme or reason. I suspect, because of all the floating crust activities by the syndicate members upstream of them, that the Long Run chub had seen, and eaten, an awful lot of crust with no fear of capture for at least two summers. Unfortunately for all of us, fishing regularly upstream we had known nothing about it but, on reflection, perhaps it was good fortune as here was a sanctuary full of big chub, confident in taking crust after two summers' free supply – and only I knew about it, until I told Neil, the man who had put me on to the stretch in the first place.

I have to say that I netted one of my best-ever bags of chub that day – nine fish between 3lb 3oz and 4lb 12oz, in fact up to that time my second-best ever. It was a truly tremendous day and I had never known happier, more absorbing, exciting fishing in all my life. I cannot think of any fishing that has combined these things as well as those sessions of at least twelve years ago. My technique that first day had been simply to introduce two or three loose crusts and wait for them to be taken. As I was forced to stand at the head of the run, I had to manipulate the bait to take whatever line was needed to cover the area of attack. No amount of drag on the bait appeared to upset the chub, as long as it was no closer than 10 yards to them.

5lb 4oz, taken from a featureless stretch of river.

My second visit I recall equally as vividly as the first. Living as I did in the coastal town of Woodbridge in Suffolk, I was pleased to be able to leave work at 3 p.m. It was another sultry, stiflingly hot day without a breath of wind, even by the sea. I visited the town's superb bakery and came away with three still-warm crusty loaves of farmhouse white that tasted so good I ate half of one during the journey to the river. Their aroma filled the car as I sped off for an afternoon's assured sport.

I think it was Bernard Venables who once declared that there was no feeling in angling quite like being taken by surprise at the sheer wonder of catching a good fish when you least expected it. It was certainly Richard Walker who retorted that, to him, there was no excitement greater than the anticipation of *knowing*, as you walked to the water, that good sport with big fish was assured. I had experienced the feeling described by Venables on more than one occasion, but it did not compare to the excitement I felt at walking across the floodplain in high summer to big chub that were guaranteed.

Things developed slightly differently that day, but in no way was the quality of sport diminished by the education I'd had during my day with them a few days previously. With line well greased and filled to the absolute maximim I had taken the advice of fellow-chubber Arthur Clarke, and polished the lip of the spool in order to reduce the friction on the line by as much as possible, thus enabling the current to draw line off the spool as easily as possible. I also polished the inside of the chrome rod rings for the same reason. I was aware that the chub were easy fish, but it's often the little sophistications to tackle that see the downfall of the biggest, wariest fish. I had teamed up the reel, a deep-spooled Mitchell 410A with spool screwed tight (none of this slipping clutch nonsense for me, I'm afraid), with a rather powerful 13-foot match rod. The choice of rod was made for four main reasons. First, the fact that I was forced to fish from the top bends' firmer ground necessitated as long a rod as possible, as it was positioned slightly away from where I really wanted to stand. The second reason was that nothing can mend line, or pick it up like a good quality match rod, and after all, was I not long-trotting in principle in any case? Third, netting fish was a case of using an extremely long telescopic landing net pole due to the inaccessibility of the bank, and every inch on the rod was an advantage. Last, it is damned exciting playing Wensum chub on a match rod! I have found few fish in the Wensum that cannot be tamed on 5lb test Maxima, and it was with this combination that I began the day.

Some of the reedy islands, I later found, were in fact quite firm and I began to know them well. It was from one of these that a couple of pretty little 3½-pounders were netted within minutes of each other. Then, on a particularly ambitious trot of nigh on eighty yards, I only thought I saw the crust disappear, no splash, no swirl, no ripple even; it just sank, as if suddenly transformed to lead. No tightening of the line ensued, nothing. I wound down, convinced I was caught up. Suddenly a sharp rush left me in no doubt that it was a chub. At eighty yards or so it is difficult to judge a fish's weight by the fight, but I held the rod high and walked downstream to meet him. A good fish at such range on a pacey river like the Wensum certainly puts a bend in the rod, especially one such as I was using, and I was enjoying every second of the epic struggle going on below. I could see little point in attempting to reel such a fish against the flow and the direction of the streamer weed, hence I walked to meet it. Better for the fish and me if I netted it close where it took the bait. As I stood on a little piece of firm ground the summer chub rolled in the sunshine. Its ink-fringed fins, its ivory-edged mouth and its gold-plated scales simply glistened, as I took a sharp intake of breath – it was one of the big ones! That chub weighed 5lb

That chub weighed 5lb 9oz and remains my largest chub to date.

9oz and remains my largest chub to this day. I would, I think, be sad in a perverse sort of way if I ever bettered it.

I suppose it was at that precise moment that I realized what I had before me, something so special that I felt honoured to be part of it. Although it seems outrageously pretentious now, I genuinely felt at the time that not only was I the right man in the right place at the right time, but also that I had a role to play as Bailey did with the river's roach, as Proudfoot did with Oulton perch and as Page had done with those Marsh tench!

Although time dims the memory I am sure that it was on the third trip and at least the fifteenth fish that changes began to take place, albeit slight ones. Chub continued to smash into the clusters of free offerings as before but it suddenly became evident that my presentation had to be a little more sophisticated. After I had dunked the crust to give it casting weight, I was forced to ensure that no drag was transmitted to the bait, for if it was it would be ignored. I soon found that it was necessary to cast downstream a bit, and to do so on whatever line I thought would cover a chub. This was no real problem, but the learning capacity of those chub was impressive, in view of the general image of their being rather thick as long as you were quiet enough. Added complications like floating bits of weed, weed reaching the surface, or any other object capable of snagging the line and pulling the crust from its natural course was enough to put the chub off. It was encouraging, however, to see that whatever I threw in as free offerings, on whatever line (to run along the very edge, mid-stream or the far bank), it would be taken as enthusiastically and voraciously as ever.

As my affinity with the floating crust method for those Long Run chub increased with each trip, I soon found myself doing little things to improve presentation without hardly realising. It soon became clear to me that, when surface crusting, it is vitally important to ensure that a belly of line does not form and precede the hookbait. I avoided this to the best of my ability by checking the line as it left the spool ever so slightly with my index finger. Two major disadvantages are created when line is allowed to accelerate past the bait. First, the natural drifting action of the crust is hindered, as the current tends to pull the crust off its course as well as increase its speed. Second, in the event of a crust being taken when the rig is behaving in this way, no direct contact to the fish is possible without having to reel in a few yards of the loop, before effecting a successful strike. You rarely get the chance as the chub will have long since felt the drag and dropped the bait.

I recall an early morning session before the afternoon shift when I suddenly and unaccountably began to miss takes, and not because of any belly in the line either. Up until then a sweeping strike upon the swirl beneath the crust as a chub took the bait was all that was needed. Timing the strike became necessary in order to set the hook and it soon became apparent that if I did not wait for a distinct tightening of the line I simply did not connect, regardless of whether the crust had disappeared into the depths or not. It was as simple as that.

The next development was a fascinating one. The chub suddenly became selective as to which crust they would take. They had evidently decided that certain crusts were dangerous. It became apparent that lone crusts, ones drifted down by me, were ignored. I wondered if this was because the crust contained a hook, but it was not the case. As I mentioned, my usual practice was to send down a handful of crusts to establish an area of feeding chub before backing them up with a trotted down bait, and then taking a fish. This time, I experimented by sending down a lone but unattached crust; following a mass attack upon a group of other crusts by the chub, the lone crust remained untaken.

Tactics were again revised and, as always, new problems were encountered. I found that I had to drift down a crust bait amongst other baits to catch them again. It was not important for them to stay bunched up; indeed, if you throw half a dozen crusts into the Wensum they will be all over the place within a couple of minutes. No, the crust bait had to appear to be part of that loose group in order to look safe to the fish down below. Total concentration was of prime importance as I often, due to my rather short concentration span, struck at what I thought was the bait being taken when it was in fact nothing more than a free offering disappearing close to the bait.

It was all exciting stuff, but to strike at nothing did little to alleviate the chubs' natural suspicion, especially when the crust insisted on staying on the hook for a few yards on the necessary retrieve. It was exciting in the sense that I never knew when the hookbait would be taken – it could be the first of the group, or even the last. Previously, I'd had a good idea when this would be, as I had already located feeding chub and the task of simply drifting a bait over them was a simple one, with the take being of no great surprise. This new method had me constantly on my toes, and it was tremendous when the hookbait was grabbed through the surface by a big white mouth with no warning, hint or preamble. It was doubly tremendous to see the free offerings being taken by others as I played a chub through the swirls. It gave me a boost to think that next cast would probably be a successful one too.

When the comparatively simple method of basic floating crust began to

A superbly conditioned Wensum chub of 4lb 12oz.

lose its appeal I became distraught, for I enjoyed no other method more. None was as exciting and gripping, or as successful, on that particular stretch of the Wensum. It has always been a mystery to me why this should be so. I attempted to repeat my success on the Waveney but I cannot remember ever getting a Waveney chub to take a surface-fished crust. No, I had to think of ways to increase the longevity of my favourite method, if only for my own sake.

A chance to do so came one afternoon when a big-looking chub appeared to slap at a piece of crust with its tail, presumably in an effort either to detect whether the crust had a hook embedded in it or, knowing that this was the case, to break up the crust and consume the resulting fragments as they sunk unattached. I have no idea if either was actually the case but it was rather irksome to see the chub consume the small fragments with such self-satisfied gusto! A new rig had to be thought out as this irritating one-upmanship by the old chub was slightly humiliating, especially as it was only crusts with hooks in them that received this strangely intelligent reaction.

My idea was a simple one – I would thread a piece of crust up the line to about eighteen inches from the hook, then nip a sizeable piece of flake on to the hook, compressing it just enough for it to sink. Into the up-line crust I inserted a matchstick, leaving half its length exposed; I then mounted the flake on to this exposed length of matchstick. This was the rig that I eventually cast to the crust-slapping chub and I awaited events with a keen eye. My idea seemed to make sense to me – should a chub decide to slap or simply swirl at a crust in its attempt to break it up, the piece of flake would easily fall away from the crust, thus fooling the chub into believing it was a perfectly safe, unattached fragment just falling away as before. This all sounds rather elaborate and I would hate you to to think that angling writers always get things right, but it *did* actually work – however, I am keeping my failures to myself, dear reader! Whilst the rig worked it did not do so without problems. Chub being chub, they occasionally took the crust itself and totally ignored the fact that they had previously tried to break them up. Once or twice they took the crust on the line and left the slowly sinking knob of flake! But all in all it was super fun, and even when it went wrong it was still exciting. The best chub I took this way was 4lb 15oz and I have long since lost count of the four-pounders that I have taken in this manner.

This new idea seemed really ripe for development, and without really having to I dreamed up as many permutations as possible. A variation was to slide a piece of crust up the line as before, but not to attach the flake to the

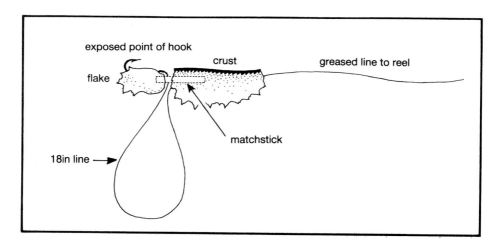

'Matchstick' rig.

crust with the matchstick. I simply left it and, in principle, 'trotted' the flake beneath the crust. The crust became the 'float', with the float doubling up as the attractor. It was splendid fun seeing the crust kite across the stream as the flake beneath it was taken. It became a source of amusement to me whenever one of these rigs worked and I was constantly uttering to myself, 'I don't believe it, it actually works!'

Another variation to the floating crust theme was the use of two fragments of crust placed apart up-line to act as a decoy, with the flake still following beneath. Throughout all this innovation I was of course still introducing lots of free crusts that continued to be taken in a serious fashion; it was just that the hooked crusts were not.

Another rather elaborate rig that brought success was a three-hook affair

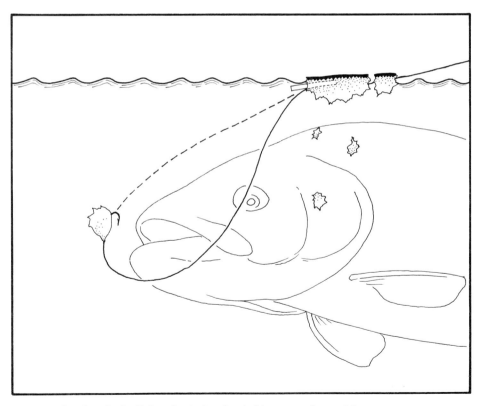

The result of a chub 'flake-slap' slowly sinking together with fragments of crust.

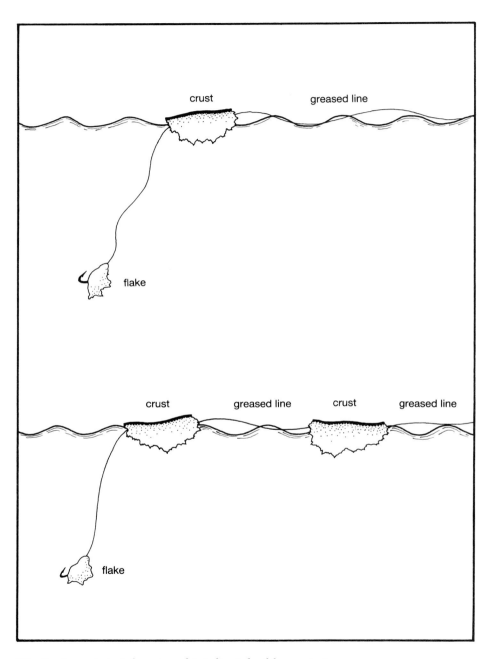

'Up-line' crust rig (above) and 'up-line' double crust rig (below).

all attached to separate crusts. I was anxious to get them taking off the top again and I believed that three crusts all trotted in a small, compact group would give the method a new lease of life. I began to reduce the size of crust too – casting three dunked crusts made a horrendous splash anyway. The chub really went for the three closely fished but small crusts in a big way. This method, like all the rest, however, began to lose its effectiveness after a few chub were caught on it. Predictably, it eventually happened that whatever form of floating crust I used, I caught nothing. Crust had been totally exhausted, it seemed. Then I made a discovery that was to blow the stretch apart once again. It was so simple that I wondered why I had not thought of it myself. Credit must go, however, to that master chubber Arthur Clarke who gave me the idea. Not believing him at first, I have to admit, I eventually took his advice, and went floating crust fishing again – at night!

When I initially considered using floating crust at night, I quickly decided it was virtually impossible; but was it? Was I not so conversant with night fishing for other species throughout the county that I rarely even used a torch? With practice could I not at least become competent?

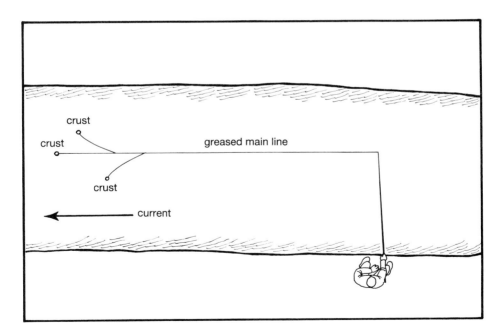

Three-hook crust rig.

I chose a still, partially overcast and yet quite moonlit, night. The day had been supremely hot, the valley had heard the hum of the insects throughout the daylight hours, and the river appeared to cut a swathe through the parched, dusty, hazy floodplain. Harvest time had arrived in East Anglia and the distant whine of the combine harvesters had abated for the day as I arrived at the Long Run expectant, but sceptical, I admit.

I threw in a half a dozen crusts. Keeping low I followed their dark shapes downstream as they floated upon the silvery sheen of the silent, muscular surface of the Wensum. It was dramatic when it came – the moonbeams flooded the scene and suddenly the crusts began to disappear amidst boils, swirls and splashes. With heart racing I flicked a crust a few yards upstream of the fast-subsiding ripples. It was all over very quickly, a take not dissimilar to that of a carp ensued and the arc of the rod was a silhouette against a backdrop of silvery rays from the by now enormous harvest moon.

Not for the first time during that campaign I uttered to myself, 'I don't believe it, it actually works!' I will never forget gazing down upon that loveliest of chub as it lay on the folds of the steaming net – 5lb 5oz of perfectly formed chub, obviously a new, uncaught fish, which I had just taken on floating crust, and at night! If ever I have owed a fish to anybody, I owed that one to Arthur Clarke.

The prime time for these nocturnal activities was two hours after sunset, which in August means about 10 p.m. An ideal time when one considers the pub licensing laws, I feel! The river would never do much after these two hours or so, at least to surface baits; but that was how I wanted to catch them, so I never stayed later to try anything else.

The technique of floating crust at night came easily to me and there is little I can add to what I have already said about the daylight methods. The cloak of darkness did little to hinder things, but moonlit nights were vastly superior for two main reasons: first, I could see the crust to strike it when taken; and second, the chub could see the crust easier themselves.

After the sheaves had all been gathered the rains came and the river never cleared itself again that summer. My floating crust obsession was forced to a close but I had done well, taking three five-pounders, countless fours, and interestingly, a smaller number of threes. The lessons I learned fishing the Long Run have held me in good stead elsewhere when I have been faced with finicky, crust-loving chub.

THE ALDER TREE RAFT SWIM

The Alder Tree Raft Swim was situated on a sharp bend on the Wensum at Drayton. The alder was a large, very mature, knarled old specimen whose branches trailed in the water during the winter and whose leaves afforded shade for the denizens beneath it during the summer months. The old tree was on the fishing bank, fortunately (the opposite bank was private), and on the outside of the bend. The current used to hit the tree roots, and had done so for many years. The bank was very undercut there and the old tree actually leaned a little into the river due to its rather shaky base. A mass of tangled, tough old roots were exposed beneath the surface, and just behind these a dead slack piece of water existed which, especialy during the winter, was covered by a raft of river debris. This was a chub swim, *par excellence*.

A fellow-contributor to this volume, fishery scientist Richard Smith, recently told me that whilst diving this particular swim one July he found chub packed into this undercut bank like proverbial sardines. To an angler standing on the bank and looking into the swim it would appear devoid of fish; little would he know that they are packed together beneath his feet.

This was a chub swim par excellence.

43

This, then, was one of my favourite winter chub swims, and one from which a good bag of fish was always possible. There is a certain *modus operandi* to get the very best out of such a swim. It does not always work, at least not for me, but its logic is sound, and on one February day of mild, grey shades, close, almost humid mists, and constantly dripping branches of endless dew, the tactic really sorted them out. Let me tell you of it.

In my experience it seems that a shoal or group of chub is made up of all sorts of fish ranging from between 2½ and 5½lb, and by the odd fish either side of this range. Roach, on the other hand, tend to be more year-class orientated. In view of these wide-ranging weights it occurred to me that there must be a pecking order of sorts, and it was my sincere belief that I could exploit this to my advantage in order to get to the fish I really wanted – the 4½lb-plus fish. I was under no illusion that virtually all the chub in the swim had felt the metal of the hook at some stage of their lives, and that I would not be dealing with uncaught fish as I had been at the Long Run stretch for instance. I deduced that in a shoal of chub such as the one that lived beneath the Alder Tree Raft Swim, with such a cross-section of fish sizes, the fish of between 3 and 4lb would virtually always be first to a bait. It seemed ludicrous to me to begin by fishing the raft itself, as it would no doubt produce a few such fish and render the bigger boys jittery enough to ignore any bait I put to them. No, I had to find a plan to preserve the raft for as long as possible, but at the same time eliminate the lesser, unwanted fish. I therefore decided to explore the concept of using the tendency of the smaller fish to be the first to a bait by attracting them *away* from the raft, their place of residence, and catching them elsewhere, thus preseving the raft for the bigger fish.

The ten yards or so of water that leads up to the raft sees a lovely straight crease about five feet from the bank. This crease is situated on the near bank and runs adjacent to the bank all the way down to the raft itself. The water inside this crease is slightly slacker than the main body of the river, and it was the ideal run to draw the smaller chub from the raft and into open water.

I began the session by introducing free samples of bread flake along the line of the crease at a point about five yards upstream from the raft, and continued to do so for the next ten yards before settling down fifteen yards upstream of the raft. At this point I introduced about half a loaf of mashed bread via a bait dropper, which would rest on the bottom, and which I hoped would appear to the chub to be the source of the food that they had followed up from beneath the raft.

The mashed bread would, I knew, hold the bottom on the inside of the

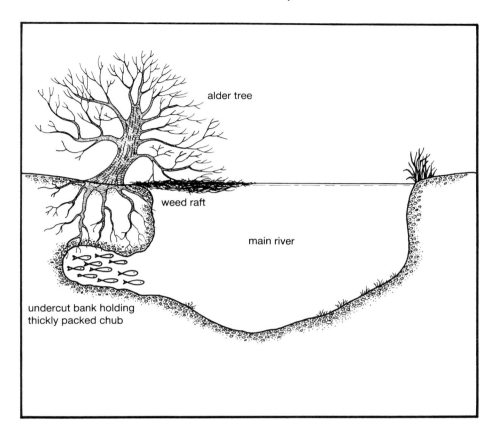

Cross-section of the Alder Tree Raft Swim.

crease line, and when found by the foraging chub I knew it would be taken avidly by them *away* from where I ultimately wanted to fish. To me, the logic was simple, as a very important objective would be accomplished by this simple tactic – the 'unwanted' smaller chub could be eliminated from the main shoal without any disturbance whatsoever to the big, less mobile fish of the raft. It was my intention to work up to these bigger fish by a series of eliminations. Not using a sprat to catch a mackerel, more like catching a sprat so that I could then catch a mackerel . . .

The river that day was carrying about six inches of visibility and was at least a foot above its normal level. I felt confident. It was, I recall, only about twenty minutes into that session when the quivertip suddenly yanked round. The 4lb test line and stout quivertip rod was sufficient for me to hustle the three-pounder quickly and without bother into the net and out of harm's way fifty yards upstream. Not believing in keeping fish in nets or sacks unless of vital importance, I watched it disappear into the brown murk and as it did so I derived smug satisfaction from the knowledge that the wheeze was beginning to take shape. I managed to take two more chub of similar stature in the next half an hour, and the little scamps were also transported well out of harm's way. I fished on for another half an hour, but I had, it seemed, lured the only three chub I could from the confines of the raft.

Throughout that little session I had continually flicked lumps of flake in so that they rolled enticingly down beneath the raft. I did this for two reasons: first, I wanted to draw as many of the smaller, easier fish upstream to me as possible; and second, if the flake was not taken by these smaller fish, the bigger chub inside the undercut bank and out under the raft would be feeding on the free samples with ever-increasing confidence.

Phase two of the operation was to move *below* the raft and tree. I had been fortunate enough to observe a shoal of chub in clear water in the summer months, which behaved in a very strange way when similarly being

A winter bag to 4lb 10oz taken from beneath a raft.

fed with lumps of flake from a point upstream. The majority of the voracious underlings had been quite content to move upstream to the source of the supply, but a number of similar-sized fish had remained where they were, allowing the rolling lumps of flake to pass them by, before turning round and taking off downstream, and devouring the bread upon catching it up. The main body of chub, the better fish, would evidently eye the antics of the younger, less experienced cousins with wry smiles, I would wager, as they remained stoically where they were.

I have no idea why the small chub should fall into two distinct groups (i.e. upstream foragers and downstream raiders), but it was clearly so and I felt, not for the first time in my life, totally confused by the ways of fish.

I therefore thought it a prudent idea to give the downstream run a look to see if any of the little chaps had mounted downstream raiding parties after the rolling balls of flake so beloved of them. I began phase two by changing the light link-leger to a heavier ¾oz bomb. I crept up to the tail end of the raft and gently dropped the rig beneath its trailing edge before settling down about ten yards below it. I was therefore upstream legering the swim, one of my favourite methods. I resolved to give the bait five minutes before raising the tip of the rod, moving the bomb and letting it bounce downstream

A drop-back bite produced this 4lb 8oz Wensum chub.

towards me for about a yard or so before repeating the process until it arrived at my feet. The flake, if pressed on to the hook hard enough, will remain attached thoughout such a manoeuvre, especially in the cold water. This bouncing flake from an upstream approach is a deadly method for Wensum chub, as they love a moving bait – it appears almost as if they are insulted by the sight of free food passing them by unmolested. I was still confident that the better chub would remain in the sanctuary of the raft and undercut bank, and that one or two smaller ones would follow the bait downstream. Upstream legering usually causes bites to be 'drop-back' affairs with the quivertip suddenly springing back, but it was not uncommon for a chub to take the flake and rush off upstream with it, giving a more conventional pulling round of the tip, which is eminently more hittable.

I was quite surprised to take a further three chub, with the best fish an encouraging 4lb 1oz, all from below the raft. I missed two drop-back bites, with the four-pounder being the only fish to belt off upstream towards the raft; was it one of the less mobile specimens? I now had six small(ish) chub safely taken from both beneath and above the raft, without any disturbance whatsoever to the raft itself. The odds were now far more favourable to take a few better fish from underneath the raft. Six what I could call nuisance fish, in this context, were eliminated and the resident better-class chub were hopefully feeding with a degree of confidence on all the flake that had been drifted down to them during my stay.

It was at last time to begin the serious session. I tingled with expectancy as I moved back upstream of the tree and raft, and cast to the lip of the collected debris, allowing the current to swing the bait (I had reverted to a link-leger again) beneath the raft and as close to the undercut entrance as possible. The quivertip took on a slight arc and my hand rested on the corks. The trap was set, I could do no more – it was up to fate now.

It was within a minute that the quivertip shot round in characteristic chub fashion and the fish was on. Kiting across the stream and away from the raft it went, but this first rush was its best and soon a sandy-coloured back broke surface waiting to be netted. At 4lb 6oz I was extremely satisfied with the gradual improvement of the fish as the plan advanced. Within ten minutes I was playing this fish's twin, and this more or less confirmed that what I was doing was exactly right for the swim.

Suddenly a much gentler, delicate bite was struck at and what I thought was a small chub soon turned out to be as perfect a roach as I have ever seen at 2lb 2oz. He looked rather startled at his quite harsh treatment whilst being played, and if I had caught no other fish that day I would have packed up feeling the whole thing had been a success. But chub continued to fall,

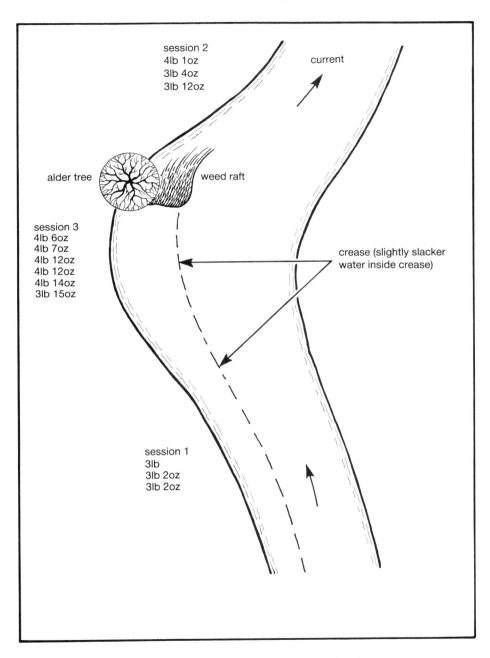

session 2
4lb 1oz
3lb 4oz
3lb 12oz

current

alder tree

weed raft

session 3
4lb 6oz
4lb 7oz
4lb 12oz
4lb 12oz
4lb 14oz
3lb 15oz

crease (slightly slacker
water inside crease)

session 1
3lb
3lb 2oz
3lb 2oz

Analysis of the Alder Tree Raft Swim experiment (overhead view).

and although I abhor a monotonous list of fish weights I feel it is important to give one in this case. A diagram of the swim which displays these weights but, more importantly, displays them exactly where the fish were taken is shown on page 49. This is a most revealing breakdown, I am sure you will agree, and fully justifies the tactics I used on the day.

Not since that memorable day has the breakdown been so marked, I have to admit, but the general trend is as I have depicted here. It has surprised me, however, how well at times the point immediately downstream of the raft fishes. I have on more than one occasion taken the best fish of the day from this often-neglected piece of water. It is also interesting to note that I have never caught a five-pounder beneath a raft. Obviously many people have, but my experience suggests that the biggest chub of all often live in the more open, ostensibly featureless runs that are often ignored by the roaming chub-hunter.

Never again, though, will I know the excitement of casting a bait to the lip of that great raft and feeling the current push the tackle deep beneath it, never again will I experience one of the many four-pounders that used to live there pull the old tip round and charge off in rage at being fooled again. The Anglian Water Authority chainsawed the old alder down to its roots. To have simply pruned the overhanging branches would have been a great loss but would have served exactly the same purpose, with the tree still, at least, in existence. But no, 'level it' is their policy, and level it they did!

Chub still haunt the undercut bank of course, but the raft is long gone. If you are not careful you can stub your toe on the remains of the stump, and the swim is nowhere as good as it once was. Whenever I walk that stretch of the Wensum, which these days is rare, I cannot do so without sitting on the old alder stump and recalling that dark, mild February day when one of my plans actually worked; and it is hard to accept that neither I nor anybody else will ever be able to repeat it.

THE GRAVEL RUN SWIM

Much of what I have written concerns the late 1970s, but in 1982 I first came across the Gravel Run Swim, and there I learned a lesson or two. At the end of a long deep glide on the Wensum the river entered a spinney and shallowed up considerably to three feet. Streamer weed waved in the faster current and between two massive beds of this weed was a gravel run of some six feet in length and about two feet across. Such was the lushness of the weed that it completely engulfed the whole run for a few seconds, before

A splendid Wensum chub of 5lb 9oz caught by Alan Rawden.

opening out again and momentarily revealing a number of good chub, until they moved beneath the weed and out of sight.

This swim was the subject of my first-ever published article, which Bruce Vaughan ran in the sadly missed and defunct *Coarse Fishing Monthly*. Below is my account.

The July day dawned red and moist. Waking at 3 a.m. I imagined the swirling mists hugging the river, and decided to pass over the chance of some more rudd. As I walked down the bridleway towards the river I looked forward to a day in the company of my chubbing rod, the dragonflies and, hopefully, some chub. The prospect pleased me. The weed-cutters, great naturalists that they are, had been and gone, and trotting was possible in certain areas – but only just.

I located a shoal of chub, suddenly, beneath my feet. The eight fish, all between 4lb and 5lb, lay facing the eternal current, occasionally jockeying each other for some unknown advantage. They looked impregnable, and so they nearly proved to be. A slug freelined would surely do the trick, I thought, if only I had some! My tackle bag, containing several baits, lay a few yards upstream but I did not want to risk spooking the chub by retrieving it. Fortunately, I managed to conjure up a knob of flake from a

A favourite swim produced a cracking fish at 5lb 6oz.

pocket. I squeezed this on to the hook and surreptitiously flicked it a good distance upstream of the shoal. The fluffy white ball rolled and swayed naturally towards the fish, and my anticipation reached its climax with the flake only a yard away from their white, leathery lips. Suddenly every chub shot off into the sanctuary of the mid-river streamer weed. The weed swayed gently from side to side and completely hid the lot of them.

Now I had caught many, many chub from that particular stretch before, on flake, crust and various other baits. Perhaps I had hammered them a bit too much, though the stretch was far removed from the usual swims that produce so many big fish each year. Undaunted, I continued on my usual beat downstream. A favourite swim produced a cracking fish of 5lb 6oz, on freelined flake. The same method went on to produce two more fish between 3lb and 4lb later in the day, and that was sufficient to restore my shaken confidence.

But that spooked shoal bothered me – how many chub had bolted at the sight of my favourite bait before? I just had to return to that swim, and when I did the fish were back. I had managed, purely by chance, to find that most marvellous of chub baits – black slugs. I tried introducing small sections of slug ten yards upstream. My calculations proved to be correct for a change – as the sections came to rest in the main swim an occasional flash of bronze indicated that the fish were at last showing an interest. To cut a long story short, I eventually took a fish after dark, while quivertipping ten yards from the feeding area. But I felt ill at ease – I could not really adjust my mind to fishing slugs on the river. It seemed a bit of a shame, an unexpected, irritating complication. I still believed that, overall, crust and flake were by far the most productive baits on the river, yet I now had to admit that a percentage of fish would bolt for cover at the mere sight of flake, however naturally it was presented. It was then that I began to think I had become a shade too mechanical, too blinkered in my approach. Perhaps if I varied things occasionally I could touch fish that I had always missed before. The fish I managed to catch on a slug section weighed a pleasing 4lb 6oz and was in perfect condition – so much so that I wondered if it had ever been out of the water in its life.

As the summer progressed I continued with my campaign for rudd – my favourite fish, if nobody else's! Consequently, it was not until October that I returned to those chub. I had decided to devote the whole month to that easily scared shoal just to see how big some of them were. I began, as before, by trickling slug sections into the run where I had caught the 4lb 6oz fish. I then left the spot for a couple of hours. The river was in good condition, but it was impossible actually to see whether the shoal was present in the usual holding area. I guessed that they were. As I wandered off downstream, passing the time-trotting flake in the spinney, I reflected on a wonderful summer. Close season ambitions had been realised and I had caught tench, bream and rudd consistently. It had been a summer in which a personal best Waveney chub had been captured after I had decided, in the close season, to ignore all chub! And there were more surprises to come.

There is usually a day during October when it suddenly dawns on me that the summer is all but over; a day when I begin to get excited about pike, roach and chub. That day I went wandering was one such.

The trotting session had been unproductive, but I did not particularly care. The pre-baited swim was the ace up my sleeve – and I knew it, as I trudged back across the water meadows. It was nearly dusk as I settled into my low chair. A barn owl perched on the skeleton of an elm tree on the opposite bank. The link-leger swung round in the heavy current, eventually settling in the pre-baited area. The quivertip took on its natural curve and the betalite upon it glowed brighter in the gathering darkness. The sun eventually disappeared into the well-wooded Wensum valley where, so my grandfather used to tell me, it slept overnight. The retiring sun released its traditional autumnal mists, which rolled gracefully down the valley, en-veloping both the swim and me. The wise bird saw fit to take its leave. A gentle pluck to the tip resulted in a nice fish of about 3lb 12oz, as bright and clean as a new pin. I re-cast, and then it happened. It was a classic gentle pluck followed by a steady pull. The rod took on its beautiful curve as the fish bored into the brown streamer weed, charged over to the far bank, boiled on the surface and then shook itself like a demon possessed as I conveyed it from water to air with the aid of steaming, dripping micromesh.

As she lay helpless and gasping under the Avons I read off the weight – 5lb 8oz, a personal best on the quivertip. She was in mint condition; I had caught five-pounders before and they had often been mishandled, it seemed, by experienced and inexperienced anglers alike. This fish was totally different. It seemed absolutely amazed at having been caught, as if it was something that only happened to lesser fish!

I knew I had been lucky, very lucky in fact. The shoal remained in the swim for a couple more weeks, then vanished. I never had another bite there, and unless the fish return I never shall. I knew, however, that I had taken the best of them!

This was how I described the Gravel Run Swim days. The Gravel Run Swim was in fact part of 'The Bushes' syndicate stretch which I had joined a few years before. Virtually all the other lads had stopped fishing there and I was

Occasionally, I would see the heron-like Alan Rawden roaming the opposite bank.

fortunate in the fact that I had the place more or less to myself. Occasionally I would see the heron-like Alan Rawden roaming the opposite bank, taking good fish here and there before disappearing like mist, but apart from that premier chub hunter, I saw nobody.

What I found interesting about those Gravel Run chub was that whilst chub were caught time and time again on bread upstream at Costessey, and had the battle-scars to prove it, these boys appeared virgin fish, afraid of bread. Bread was hardly unknown to them, surely. It had been thrown into the stretch for years, but somehow they were just not switched on to it. Since I wrote that article I have returned to the swim and when the river is clear, on a fine summer's day, the streamer weed will part and I can still see a shoal of pristine chub. Bouncing through bread still frightens them, luncheon meat is incapable of producing any reaction at all and cheese, probably because of its colour, scares them as much as bread. Perhaps the chub are like me, and run a mile at the sight of white sliced supermarket bread.

No, natural baits always worked best, be they slugs (obviously), lobs, frogs and, once, even a grasshopper. I would have loved to have used crayfish but at that time they were rare in the Wensum and it did not seem right. Crayfish are, however, making a bit of a comeback and I would love to try them now.

THE SPINNEY

At the tail of the Gravel Run begins the Spinney. The Spinney has in fact been neglected for years and in high summer walking through it is no easy matter. It was in the Spinney that I tried a little experiment which was to prove very interesting. Between 1979 and 1982 I did very little chub fishing, but finding the Gravel Run Swim and seeing good chub on the bank brought the old feelings back again. Back to my early article:

Further interesting facts came to light during the summer. As an experiment I fished floating crust, but did not feed free samples first. I wanted to avoid crusts drifting downstream at regular intervals or as a group. It had usually

Seeing good chub on the bank brought the old feelings back again.

been a habit of mine to loose-feed crust initially, and then to fish the spot where they had been taken. As I said, I had decided to fish floating crust with no free samples at all, and the results from the few trips I made during the summer were certainly encouraging. The chub appeared to have no fears if a single crust drifted down alone. But if a hooked crust went down with other pieces, the whole flotilla would be ignored like the plague. In fact, it even appeared that a group of crusts, with no hooked piece in the midst of them, would be ignored as well.

Perhaps at this stage I ought to say why I decided to try this single-crust technique. The best way to do this is probably to take a look at the results of the first experimental session, which produced chub of 5lb 6oz, 4lb 2oz and 3lb 15oz, in that order. The order is the key. If, for example, I had initially introduced the usual free samples, singly even, I think that the first free crust would have been taken by the five-pounder. In fact, I do not believe that the five-pounder would have taken anything other than that first crust. I have heard a lot about 'pecking orders' in the fish world and I agree wholeheart-edly with this concept. It certainly explains why the biggest fish tend to get first go at a bait. (I have known for years the first crust to be sent down would be the safest, and that the big, wise old chub knew it.) As I said earlier, throwing in a few free samples will get the big fish taking confidently but if you then trot a crust down you will probably catch the smaller fish. Big chub, being what they are, soon wise up and realise that the two or three samples of food coming downriver are going to be the safest. I had suspected this to be the case for some time, hence my little experiment during the summer. Could that first trip have been a mere coincidence? Well yes, but further trips had me believing otherwise. The bigger fish did tend to come first. Mentally, fish are pretty stupid things; they live by their instincts, and they can be fooled time and time again if the angler can keep one step ahead of them. Fish *must* feed, and it is always worth remembering this when sport is slow. You always have the advantage.

When looking back on previous articles, one notices that opinions are usually slightly different, but what I wrote then holds true today. It is interesting to compare the 'pecking order' of the crust-taking chub as described above and those of the Alder Tree Raft Swim, where it was reversed. I think the key is to try to understand what is going on below and fish accordingly, rather than to follow a proven, yet limited, method slavishly through thick and thin.

An early shot of Alan Rawden learning his trade – this chub was 4lb 14oz.

PIKE CORNER

On the Waveney in 1972 there was a dark, tree-hidden, nettle-ridden, snag-ridden, plug-ridden bend known locally as Pike Corner. I recall my first sight of it well, having been taken there by a seventeen-year-old farm worker from my grandfather's farm. He told me of the 'bottomless hole' where monster pike lurked and chub cruised the surface as big as cod.

Although the day was bright and warm, the instant I entered the cloak of tall trees the gloom and cooler air hit me. It was indeed a mysterious place and it was a strange sensation to be guarded by acres of vicious stinging nettles; I suppose the place represented every boy's dream – an impenetrable den!

The choice was pike or chub, and I have to confess, chub lovers, that if my pocket money had stretched to a plug, pike would have been the choice, but a tub of split shot and half a dozen size 8 gilt hooks was the only equipment within my financial grasp, so it was with those that I set up a rig for these cod-like chub! Looking back on the day now I am impressed with myself for using luncheon meat as bait at such a tender age.

Pike Corner was in reality a wonderful chub swim, and I shall never forget, at the very edge of the trees, swaying hypnotically over 'cabbages', a shoal of enormous roach that were totally, utterly, 100 per cent uncatchable. How I wish I had teamed up with my present fishing partner then, that wily old roach-fishing sage – J.B.!

Just upstream of the swim the Waveney was fast and ran over gudgeon-infested gravel before hitting the bend beneath the trees. Here, the flow was deflected along the outside of the bend before settling down to a nice, easy glide to the weeping willows where shoals of immense roach again resided. A small raft of rubbish had collected at the point where the current hit the bank, and the method was an obvious one.

My reference books had told me that to hold back an Avon float would make the bait swing outwards and upwards, and to me it seemed to be the best method to see if any of these 'cod' could be caught from this bend. The cast was made and as the float tackle chuntered towards the deflected water I held back and caused the bait to swing round and search the depths below, whether they be bottomless or not. The Avon float, so good for trotting large baits, sailed under and a chub which I suspect was around 3½lb caused great excitement between the apprentice farm worker and myself, ensconced as we were amongst the trees of gloom.

The memory of that fish's fight has been dimmed by time but it was jolly arm-aching, I can tell you; we whooped, we shouted, we cheered, and the fact that this was the first Waveney swim I ever showed my Wensum informant, Neil, has always caused a rather romantic notion on my part that my whole chub fishing career is intrinsically linked from swim to swim to ultimate Utopia.

The beauty of the Pike Corner swim was that you could always guarantee a chub there; to trot the float fished bait-down, to hold back and let the bait swing round beneath the bank would always produce a chub first cast. But that was always it – never have I taken two chub from that swim in a day, and I have to admit that the Pike Corner swim would never be quite the same again if I did.

THE PIPE SWIM

On a singularly uninteresting stretch of the Wensum a gas pipe was laid which ran through the floodplain, across the river and off towards the village. A small concrete notice has been erected stating that this is so, and it is beside this somewhat incongruous little object that some of my best bags

A singularly uninteresting stretch.

of chub have been taken. In the winter this particular swim acts like a magnet to chub, with odd roach and bream also muscling in.

This swim is so good because as the pipe was being laid, a trench was dug in the river bed with the pipe duly being laid in it. When the pipe was covered up again a depression formed in the contours of the bed at this point, which in effect took on the appearance of a six-foot strip across the bottom. This was easily visible during the summer months, but nowhere near so obvious in the winter. During the summer it appeared to hold very little and was often ignored by all, but with a bit of plumming when the river was coloured, a real chub hot spot could be unearthed.

Accurate feeding and casting was, I found, essential for this swim, and I suspect why many anglers failed there was because their approach was too sloppy for the crucial area one had to fish in order to achieve results. My whole approach to fishing is rather sloppy, I must confess, but it was that little gas symbol on the bank that told me exactly where I should feed and then fish. I always used one of angling's greatest inventions when feeding up this swim – the humble Thamesley bait dropper. What I did in fact was to take two rods down to the swim – one for the sole purpose of introducing

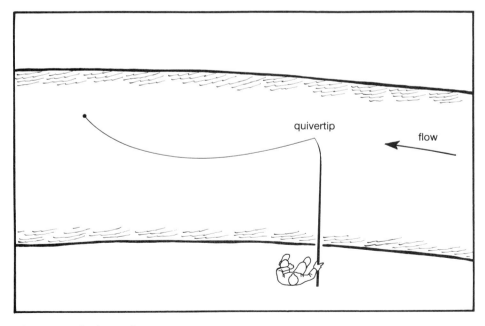

The arc in the line when using a quivertip.

61

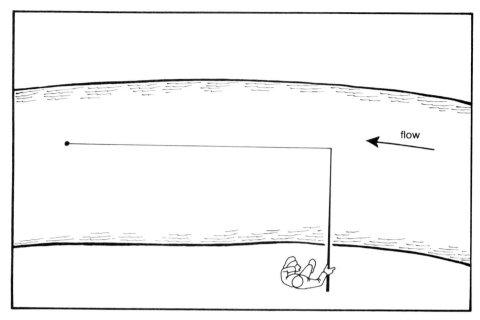

The arc straightened when rod-tip legering is employed.

bread via the bait dropper throughout the session, and the other for fishing with. It never appeared to bother the chub at all when I cast out the rather heavy, noisy bait dropper, and bites would continue as before whenever I used it. Indeed, I shall never forget a chub grabbing the bait dropper on the retrieve on one occasion when it had failed to open! I distinctly recall 'playing' the fish for several seconds before it let go; it was at that point that I decided the bait dropper hardly filled them with acute fear.

As it ran over the Pipe Swim the river was faster than usual and, whilst the chub were very obliging there, problems were encountered with the bites-to-fish ratio. Due to the swamp-like nature of the bank it became necessary to fish further upstream than I would have liked. Fifteen yards was as close as I could get to the depression caused by the pipe, and when you have that much line being pushed around by the current it is difficult to have a direct pull on the fish as it takes the bait. I was not in the position of being able to fish opposite the fish and therefore reduce the arc of the line, so I had to try to reduce the missed bites I was getting from my position way upstream.

I well recall the day when a piece of misfortune suddenly became a lucky break, literally, as I stumbled and fell. Upon getting back on my feet I was devastated to see that the Drennan quivertip was broken at the screw-in base. I almost decided to drive staight to Norwich and buy a replacement as I had none in the tackle bag, but I am so glad that I did not. Forced as I was to rod-tip leger I suddenly found that the increase in resistance to a taking chub caused far more positive, aggressive and hittable bites than ever before. I also realised that to fish without the quivertip allowed me to fish tighter to the hookbait, thereby reducing the arc of the line in the water. Ordinarily I had used a bomb that just managed to hold bottom but that day I decided to use one of 1½oz as opposed to my normal ¾oz; this allowed me to tighten up even more to the bait. Bites suddenly became barbelesque, the rod often pivoting on the rests in response to a tearaway chub bite. It soon became apparent that the Pipe Swim was seething with chub, and the only reason that I could see for this was that depression in the riverbed.

My new tactics brought to an end the odd big roach and bream that sometimes turned up, but the bites-to-chub ratio improved beyond all expectations. It is easy to see why, of course – from the chub taking a bait and feeling a slight draw on the line before dropping it, causing me to curse as I struck into nothing above, they were taking the bait, feeling immediate and heavy reistance and bolting with it, hooking themselves through the soft bread flake and subsequently pulling the rod virtually off its rest.

I recall that at around that time I read an article concerning the sensitive bites that appeared the norm for chub these days, and how in the old days (and indeed in the old books) positive rod-wrenching chub bites were common. It is easy to realise why this was so; much of the old-style chub fishing was done by rod-tip legering, thus causing the kind of bites lamented by the article writer.

The advent of the quivertip brought an end to such bites, the chub angler now being used to more refined plucks and pulls on the sensitive, virtually resistance-free quivertips. I personally much prefer the quivertip kind of bite as I have never totally come to terms with the self-hooking bolt rig style of the rod-tip, be it with chub or with any other species. However, shock tactics like those I employed at the Pipe Swim were used because of the circumstances I have described. I do not regret it, and without such tactics my success there would have been severely reduced.

And so the party on the Wye returned, and I returned from the almost tangible fragments of memory that had so overwhelmed my thoughts that day. How could all those lovely old swims, mostly destroyed or changed now, suddenly reappear in front of me, intact and unfished? If I were born of a younger generation, would I not have had the same experiences on

And so the party returned.

those Welsh swims as I'd had years before on that opposite bulge of land to Wales – East Anglia? As we all walked back to the car I realised that there is no such thing as time, there is simply change, and if you are a lover of rivers then you will have made the cruellest choice of all, for nothing, to me, can compare to the simple concept of a river journey from source to sea and, metaphorically, from birth to death – and nothing can compare to the heartless and greedy exploitation that rivers have to suffer. Look upon a river as a life: twists, turns, deeps and shallows, tributaries, pollutants, rapids and slacks. Fight their destruction and their exploiters as you would your own. I can think of no better analogy of a river than Chris Turnbull's phrase, 'the veins of the country,' and no fish epitomise the image of the river to the vast majority of anglers that sit by them every day than the subject of this book – chub and dace.

A 'long-run' five for Miller on surface crust.

A thick-set 5lb 6oz crust-loving chub.

Bailey plays a Wye feeder-stream chub.

Darkness failed to put these chub off taking surface crust.

A Wye 'beast' boils on the surface for Miller.

Fred Sykes with his stunning 6lb 7oz Annan chub.

A Welsh chub which fell to the fly.

John Knowles of Oxford plays his first Wensum chub.

Dave Plummer's winter session was rewarded with this 5lb 5oz Wensum fish.

The baiting over, what will the night bring?

The ponded Wensum upstream of Taverham Mill – not
many chub here.

The ideal chub river – a fast flow, clean gravel and plenty of
trees.

A Year on the Cherwell

Trefor West

If ever a name has been synonymous with chub it is that of Trefor West. Arguably the finest exponent of small river chub fishing alive today, Trefor's understanding of the species is second to none. Successful on the Oxfordshire rivers and Norfolk's own river Wensum, Trefor has contributed to the angling press for several years now, in a style that at the same time informs and inspires the reader.

No book on chub could possibly be complete without a contribution from Trefor. His chapter in his book centres around the Cherwell in Oxfordshire, and he discusses summer, autumn and winter fishing on the river in his own inimitable way.

If ever a name has been synonymous with chub, it is that of Trefor West.

The Cherwell was our training ground.

Looking back over twenty-five years of chub fishing on all types of river, from small intimate streams to the powerful and majestic Avon and Stour of Hampshire, I can say that the lessons I learned about chub location and behaviour in many happy years on the Oxfordshire Cherwell have proved to be invaluable on all these various fisheries.

In the formative years of the Coventry Specimen Group, the Cherwell was our training ground. It is my intention to illustrate specific lessons which I learned, and which I consider to be of particular relevance in my progress as a chub catcher.

A SUMMER CHALLENGE

Naturally I will consider the summer season first, and the pun is intended; for summer chub I need look no further than a natural bait. Crayfish, black slug, lobworm, etc. are all engulfed greedily by 'old leather chops', provided your approach and presentation is artful enough.

Izaak Walton described the chub as the 'fearfullest of fish' and to a certain

The 'fearfullest of fish'.

extent that is true, but I have never found it necessary to crawl on hands and knees, Red Indian-fashion, to get into a casting position as I have often read advocated. Having said that, my progress upstream is slow and cautious, two or three yards back from the river edge, and at all times avoiding heavy footfalls and using the bankside vegetation to conceal my approach where possible. The ability to cast natural bait accurately to the chub you've located improves with practice and each good cast will instill more confidence in your tackle control. Good attempts at impossible casts under far-bank bramble and willow should be counted as a large proportion of the pleasure if achieved, whether a chub takes the bait or not.

My first two summers fishing natural baits were a revelation, twenty chub a day between 2lb and 4½lb being the norm; thirty-one for a total over 100lb, with eight between 4lb and 4lb 14oz, was a memorable day – it seemed that every chub in the river wanted to check out the bottom of my landing net that perfect midsummer day. It was too good to be true. I believed I could go on knocking out a dozen or so every trip for the rest of

It seemed that every chub in the river wanted to check out the bottom of my landing net.

my days. But I was in for a rude awakening. Crayfish and black slugs cast perfectly to land a couple of feet in front or behind a chub lying in mid-stream were inspected briefly and rejected. No longer would the chub smash into my bait, leaving me with just the formality of setting the hook. My catch rate dropped dramatically, refusal became the expected and frustration accompanied it. This problem was not just associated with a couple of my favourite stretches of the river, but was evident on all the venues to which I had given the crayfish treatment. Only when I located a group of fish was I reasonably confident that, because of the competition element, one of the shoal would engulf my offering. It got worse, chub bolting in terror when a crayfish dropped from the sky anywhere near them. Time for a rethink, and quick – before my pride was damaged beyond repair.

I had a vision of crayfish multiplying by the thousand as chub no longer considered them main course on the menu, armadas of crayfish herding shoals of chub into barren corners of the river, and smiles of triumph on the crayfish's faces as the chub meekly obeyed their new masters. What nonsense! Chub have eaten crayfish for generations – even chub whose river no longer contains crayfish will eat them, surely suggesting that an inbred instinct is telling the chub that the object swimming erratically past them is good to eat. 'Swimming eratically past them,' I repeated to myself. My smirk broadened into a smile as the idea expanded in my brain; a plan of action was formulated and would be implemented on the morrow. I was awake at the crack of 10 a.m.

A dozen crayfish from under the large stones in the fast-flowing shallow water by the road-bridge were unusually difficult to catch, as if they were aware that today was the start of a whole new ball game. I would find out whether it was in less than twenty minutes.

The swim a mile upstream was the obvious choice as a place in which to draw a firm conclusion about forthcoming events. The two resident chub

The largest fell to crayfish the previous season, in June, at 4lb 8oz.

were both old acquaintances; the largest fell twice to crayfish the previous season in June at 4lb 8oz and again in September at 1oz heavier. Its companion, at 3lb 13oz, was one of those short, thick-set examples of chubhood destined to be a five-pounder simply because of his shape and condition. Both had mocked my attempts to land them this summer, showing total contempt for both crayfish and slug cast perfectly to them.

I peered over the marginal nettles. The two chub were in residence, both holding position just off the main flow, two feet behind a drooping willow branch which afforded them both cover and shade. Moving well back from the river I assembled my tackle, the 6lb maxima no. 4 needle-sharp Lion d'Or hook and my 10-foot Avon rod, all of which have served me well over the years. The faultless clutch on my ABU 54 was again unnecessarily tested. A 1½in crayfish, the perfect size for casting the hook, pulled through the second segment of the tail, and the business end of the simple freeline set-up was ready. A rod line, hook and bait, two chub to fish for and the moment of truth was seconds away. I moved slowly into casting position opposite the chub, using the head-high stinging nettles for cover as the two chub remained blissfully unaware of the drama. One of them, hopefully, would soon be an unwilling participant.

The crayfish landed ten yards above the chub, directly in line with their position behind the branch. The bail arm snapped closed and the slack line was retrieved on to the reel, leaving me in direct contact with the crayfish. Keeping the rod low to the water I wound the crayfish downstream towards the two chub. The crayfish was now six inches below the surface. A yard above the chub I stopped retrieving the line and allowed the crayfish to sink to mid-water. Three six-inch downstream movements of the rod man-oeuvred the crayfish to a collision course with the chub. They both saw it at the same time and moved towards it, a six-inch twitch on the rod produced the illusion of a crayfish attempting to escape and the nearest chub gently sipped the crayfish into his huge mouth. 'You're going to eat that, aren't ya,' I said out loud to the fish. A hard upward pull set the hook, the crayfish flipped out of the chub's mouth as the hook went home, and the other chub gratefully finished the meal that his companion had obligingly decided to share.

Pulling hard downstream, the chub turned and bolted away from the danger of the willow branches. Keeping the rod low I grabbed the landing net and set off in pursuit of the hooked fish. Fifteen yards below and a few minutes later I eased the golden, brassy-flanked chub into the landing net. A smile spread across my face as I lifted my prize from the water. As the forceps nicely dislodged the hook I was sure I could detect an expression of

The forceps dislodged the hook nicely.

disbelief on the chub's face. The scale needle flickered at 4lb 12oz, 4lb 13oz, and settled at 4lb 11oz. 'Nice one, Cyril,' my largest chub of the summer so far. Twenty minutes later the first chub's companion registered 4lb 1oz on the scale after a terrific scrap. As the chub ploughed through the cabbages in mid-river, the line cut the leaves as the chub sought the sanctuary of the thick roots. Two fours in two casts on crayfish; I felt that maybe, just maybe, I was back in business.

Thirteen more chub with three more over 4lb brought the day to a satisfying conclusion. There was the hint of a spring in my step as I walked along the canal tow-path back to the car to a meal and a good, long sleep. The fifteen chub landed that day had all taken crayfish, an almost totally unacceptable bait the previous weekend. With only two or three complete rejections all day I felt I had conclusively proved, to my mind, that the crayfish was still a very desirable meal for the chub. What had been wrong was my presentation of the meal. The loud plop as the bait landed in the water near the chub in the early days was a successful and easy method of presentation, but they soon learned that the meals landing from the heavens

The needle flickered at 4lb 12oz, 4lb 13oz and settled at 4lb 11oz.

led to a hook in their mouths and a spell out of water. A crayfish presented with more thought and subtlety, in fact in the way they expect to encounter them every day, was readily acceptable. This modification to my crayfish presentation, plus the developments of the induced take, was, I felt, a significant step forward in my ability to deceive and subsequently catch summer chub.

AUTUMN PRESENTATIONS

Moving on in the chub-catcher's year to September, the chub are considerably harder to locate in their usual haunts. The river has begun to lose that lushness, and the vigorous weed and bankside growth has petered out to a pale yellowing of the summer's greenness; flows diminish and oxygen levels can change dramatically, affecting the behaviour and willingness of the chub to feed consistently. Small pockets of fish will often join up to form larger shoals and move together to the better-oxygenated sections of the river. The shallow, faster flowing sections that probably would only hold the odd two-pounder for most of the season can be frequented by a dozen or

Cheer up Trefor! 5lb 2oz isn't that bad.

more fish of all sizes seeking the extra oxygen supply they need under generally low, stale river conditions.

Approaching cautiously and presenting a bait to the shoal would most likely bring instant success, the competitive element being so high in these circumstances, but the likely outcome would also be that the rest of the shoal would be spooked and scattered in all directions, and a golden opportunity for further success missed.

A legered bait cast directly into the area from well upstream has basically the same effect, so repeated direct casts should be avoided. The situation requires that a bait be presented to the shoal from well upstream without the disturbance of a cast to them. The answer – floating crust, an exciting visual method that has the pleasing habit of sorting out the larger fish. Strangely, when the shoal switches on to the surface crusts they appear to lose some of their natural caution and I have found that provided no glaring mistakes in presentation are made they will tolerate the disturbance caused by hooked members of the shoal, at least until their numbers have diminished considerably.

One or two devious tricks in presentation can also be employed to pick off a couple more fish from a shoal that has become cautious and refuses to take the floating bait; but more of that later.

The main points to consider when floating crusts are that the crusts must reach the area of activity at the correct speed – too slow will result in refusal, and likewise a crust moving too fast will also be rejected. The most common fault and the main cause of poor surface crust presentation is insufficient line on the spool. If the line won't sneak through the rod rings, pulled off the spool by the weight of the crust and the flow of the water, your chances of a good presentation are remote. A spool loaded to within 2mm of the lip will correct that bad fault. Too fast a presentation will usually be caused by line preceding the bait, which must be avoided at all times. Checking the release of line will enable the crust to overtake the preceding line, and on release the likelihood of correct presentation will be increased tenfold. All adjustments to line and direction should be completed before the surface bait reaches the area of chub activity. The timing of the strike can be crucial – the temptation to hit the chub when your crust disappears in a huge swirl should be resisted. Instead, count to three and look for your line straightening on the surface, then give it a firm upward pull. Line grease applied to within six inches of the bait will assist line pick-up considerably, and will also allow you to see the bows and bends in your presentation that will need correction. Size 6 hooks to ten-pence-sized crust is my standard surface crust terminal gear.

*When a shoal switches to surface crusts, they appear
to lose some of their natural caution.*

The next point for consideration is the amount of loose offerings of crust to introduce into the swim. This is a difficult question to answer; it is equivalent to asking 'How long is a piece of string?' A good guide-line would be that the faster the flow, the higher the number of loose offerings that need to be introduced. The chub reaction will of course dictate to a certain degree the timing of the drift-down of the baited crust. I would normally only present my hook-crust when two or more different chub in the shoal are intercepting the loose crust. It would not, in most instances, take long, for once one member of the group has taken a crust, being greedy individuals the rest of the chub will not want to miss out on an easy meal.

My favourite Cherwell floating crust swim is typical of many rivers all over the country. The long, straight length of river above the shallows is choked full of weed and reed-mace, and the flow is negligible. The river takes a right-hand curve and shelves up to barely six inches deep. A side-stream enters fifteen yards down the shallows and the mound of silt deposited at its mouth forms a plateau which in summer reduces the river width by half, and in doing so doubles the speed of flow, channelling all the water down the far bank and under a draping willow tree. Here, the depth is

A greedy individual – a 4lb 12oz Cherwell chub.

76

increased by six inches with each yard of progress down from the side-stream entrance, the depth near and under the willow becoming 2ft 6in of the only well-oxygenated water for a mile in either direction.

On one particular visit to this stretch I jumped the side-stream well away from the river, and walked down to the hawthorn bushes opposite the far bank willow, peering through a small gap that a pair of secateurs had produced for me in the close season. I could see nine chub clearly, and two or three more dark shapes could be detected under the willow. At least two fish looked four pound-plus, the best nearer five. From my position, kneeling on the silt bed, I flicked two loose crusts into the flow and watched their progress downstream towards the willow and the shoal of chub. Two feet from the branches the crusts disappeared in huge swirls. A loose crust, followed by my hookbait, proceeded downstream. My baited crust a yard above the tree, I checked its progress by placing my finger on the spool, simultaneously lifting the line off the water and laying it straight behind the bait. With my finger taken off the spool, the crust proceeded correctly for two feet, then vanished in a swirl; the line cut through the water as the fish turned down and I pulled the hook home. Right-hand sidestrain extracted the chub from the shoal, and the rest of the fight took place in front of the bushes at the end of the plateau. The chub was soon under control and I beached it gently at my feet.

Before unhooking this one, I threw a couple of small crusts into the flow to maintain the shoal's interest and also to help calm any suspicions that may have been aroused by the departure of one of the shoal. The two crusts were taken immediately they reached the branches of the willow. I returned the chub above the shallows; 3lb 13oz, a nice start. Two loose crusts and the hook-crust again drifted down. Two takes were made to the free offerings and the hookbait was left. It lodged against the branches where the water pressure against it made it bob up and down in the water's determination to push it free. I could see a chub directly under the bread; I left it for a minute, but there was no take. A loose crust was floating two feet above the tree; I gently teased the hookbait free from the branches, and both were taken simultaneously, the chubs' backs clearing the water in their enthusiasm for the meal. Right-hand sidestrain resulted in a 3lb 9oz chub. In twenty minutes I took and returned chub of 2lb 11oz, 2lb 13 oz, 3lb 8oz, 4lb 1oz above the shallows. Three loose crusts had gone through unmolested, however, so I felt it was time for the dirty tricks brigade to put in an appearance.

I clipped a single lead-free swan-shot to the line four inches from the hook. I baited the hook with a ten-pence-sized piece of fluffy bread flake, ensuring

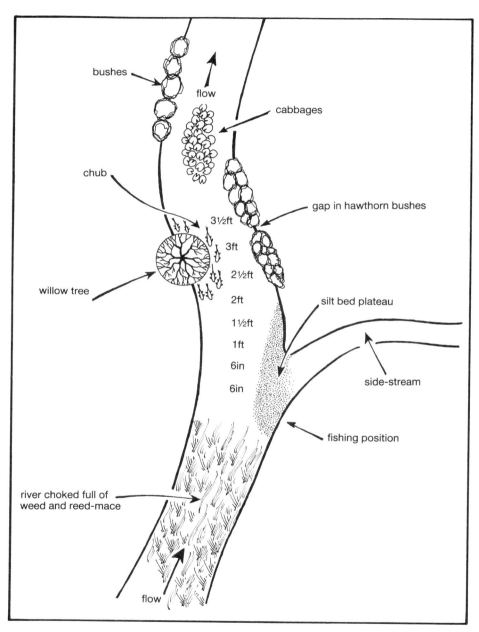

bushes

flow

cabbages

chub

3½ft

3ft

gap in hawthorn bushes

2½ft

willow tree

2ft

silt bed plateau

1½ft

1ft

6in

6in

side-stream

fishing position

river choked full of
weed and reed-mace

flow

Diagram of Cherwell surface crusts swim.

that the hook point was left exposed. The flake hookbait and swan-shot were fused to a piece of crust by gently pressing the swan-shot into the flake of the crust; just enough adhesion to enable me to flick the crust into the flow was all that I required. The crust drifted down to the tree, a gentle tug on the line momentarily checked its progress, and the flake hookbait and swan-shot detached from the crust to sink enticingly under the branches. Taking up the slack line left a nice bow from swan-shot to rod top for bite detection. The waiting time was minimal, for chub that are willing to take surface baits will find a thoughtfully presented legered bait irresistible. The line twitched and fell slack, a sweeping strike set the hook, and a large vortex appeared on the surface under the branches as my maximum right-hand sidestrain met the stubborn resistance of the chub. The rod pressure won the battle and the chub turned downstream and moved to mid-stream, stubbornly shaking his head in an attempt to release my hookhold. He's mine now, I'll not allow him to reach the willow branches again. 'He looks like a big four,' I thought, as I netted him at the tail of the plateau. A lovely-shaped, admirably firm fish, with golden flanks, coral pink fins and pefect scale formation. The scale confirmed my estimate, 4lb 12oz. He'll be 5lb 2oz or 5lb 4oz in February. 'I hope we meet then,' I thought as I gently returned him to his river. The disturbance under the tree caused by this large fish spooked the remaining fish. A biteless twenty minutes confirmed that I had extracted my last chub from the swim for that day. Time to move and locate a new group of chub to drift surface crust down to.

THE WINTER SEASON

I had learned the lesson that, by working at the shoal from well upstream with no direct casts into the group, I could pick them off and end up with a good catch and the big fish. Provided my presentation and tackle control is subtle enough they will not spook when they are interested in surface crust; a far more enjoyable and productive method than the guaranteed sure-fire one cast directly into the chub shoal.

The river held a nice tinge of colour from the rain which had fallen a couple of days previously, and the quivertip pulled round for the fourth time as my legered crust was picked up by a chub under the far bank rubbish raft. Four chub in four casts – I was in for a productive and enjoyable mild January day's fishing.

Time to move on to the next classic chub raft a quarter of a mile downstream. I stopped just before the new swim, and the thought suddenly

A lovely shaped fish.

occurred to me, 'How many chub have I just walked past on my way to the next textbook swim?' That question nagged at me for the rest of the day.

I decided that the next day I would examine these areas of what appeared to be boring, featureless lengths of river between classic chub swims. The significance of that decision was without doubt to change my whole approach to winter chub catching, and opened up miles of previously unfished water on every river I fished.

Initially the progress was slow, the odd fish turned up in areas that to my inexperienced eye appeared no different to anywhere else, therefore with no logical reason for the chub to be there. A 4lb 14oz chub inspired my determination to piece together the jigsaw of depths, flow speed, type of bottom, directional flow change etc. The permutations of possible reasons could be endless. That winter season drew to a close with many, if not all, of the questions unanswered.

A LESSON TO BE LEARNED

Mid-May close season visits to the river and a chance to look closer at these featureless sections in clear water showed me that 'featureless' was in fact a totally false description, for I found clean gravel, shelves, undercuts, drop-offs, clay boulders which deflected the flow, underwater snags of all sizes, and so on. My mind was racing in its attempt to connect each of last winter's fish to the previously unseen feature in the area that produced the bite.

Several common denominators appeared to be emerging, a certain flow speed being the most noticeable. The following winter my results trebled in these sections of river, and with each fish my confidence grew. Eventually my ace chubbing companion, Tony Miles, and I decided that the classic chub swims left much to be desired in terms of constantly producing four pound-plus fish, and we devoted more and more of our wintertime chub fishing to smooth runs and glides, and straight sections of river. We've since landed hundreds of fours and dozens of fives between us, and would now be quite content never to cast under a raft again. Of course we have not totally abandoned the classic chub swim, for to do so would be foolish. However, by fishing and working these unfished sections we are fishing for the whole river's population and not just the classic chub swim residents.

As each summer and winter went by my knowledge and confidence in these sections of river grew and the locations of swims became a formality on every river we fished. The flow direction change became the classic swim

What appeared to be boring, featureless lengths of river between classic chub swims.

*A 4lb 14oz inspired my determination to piece together the
jigsaw.*

and could be spotted from considerable distances. The steady walking-pace
flow rate adjacent to a faster water speed, which produced a clearly defined
crease between the conflicting flows, became a bite producer to match any
raft swim I had ever fished. Then out of the blue the final piece of the jigsaw
dropped into place and all the years of probing, searching and questioning
seemed to fall into a neat little pile.

The quivertip pulled round confidently; the crust bait had been settled
less than a minute in the swim, a long glide of open water which was the
main flow down the far bank. The hook pulled home and a good fish tore
off downstream. The rod in my hand took on my favourite shape, bent
double. He stopped after five or six yards of line had been taken off my ABU
54. Jigging and boring to left and right, the chub sought his freedom with a
positive determination.

I eased the fish back upstream towards the waiting landing net, a long
four minutes away from being recorded in my diary and memory bank of
pleasing captures. Then 'clunk' the fish went solid into an unseen snag.
Altering the direction of pull several times, and slackening off in the hope

A five-pounder which feel to the 'silt-bed' theory.

the fish would swim free of the obstruction of its own accord resulted in no progress whatsoever – stalemate. Keeping contact with the fish I moved downstream to try a direct pull from that direction, again to no avail. I slid down the bank to stand on a pile of silt in the margin and tried exerting pressure from directly above the snagged-solid chub. I sensed a movement below me, and a submerged tree branch with a 4lb chub attached to it broke the surface. The chub swirled angrily, the hook shot out, the half-ounce lead whistled past my head, came back just as fast on the shortline and smacked into the back of my head. A few choice words to the log, the chub, the pain in my neck, didn't make things any better at all. A long sigh of frustration was followed eventually by a smile in the realisation that you can't win 'em all.

I picked up the rod and turned to climb back up the bank, when a shiny object lying in the silt caught my eye. I bent down to pick it up for a closer examination. Nothing unusual, just half a swan mussel shell; there were several more in the silt around me. I'd noticed them before when I was landing or returning a chub. My brain engaged in a train of thought, slowly at first, then as the reasoning began to unfold with several facts it seemed that a common denominator had dropped into place. I looked at the silt bed

Classic chub swim residents.

– pea mussels' shells, hundreds of them, and grains of sand and gravel mixed with bits of shell and other water-borne debris of the same size and individual weight and consistency, all deposited together to form what I call silt beds; not rotting vegetation, leaves and weed which the river's flow pushes on to end up in the slacks with the lighter water-borne sediments, which will form together and end up as mud. The silt beds are basically made up of several different water-borne commodities all of the same weight, size and density. When the river is in full flood the extra water pressure moves the unattached debris and waste downstream in a roll-on effect; as the water level and flow rate recedes, items of the same weight and density come to rest at the same place forming silt beds, mud banks, weed rafts, etc. The silt beds are formed only where the flow rate is capable of bringing the ingredients of a certain density to a particular spot on the water course but incapable of continuing to push them downstream until the next flood; hence all come to rest in a small area of river and form the silt bed. The significance of this is that a certain flow speed and a silt bed bottom is an extremely attractive combination to winter chub. I'm 100 per cent sure in my mind that the silt bed–flow rate chub connection is a sound logical basis to work from. I've caught literally hundreds of chub from these swims over the years on every river I've fished. I'm not suggesting that every silt

Funny old game isn't it?

bed contains a dozen chub and all you have to do is cast in and then weigh
the resulting four-pounder, that would be absurd. You will still need to fish
with thought, and prepare and search the general area with a degree of
thoroughness and determination in order to suceed. I've found these areas
to be highly productive bite producers in winter and that the ability to pick
them out on lengths of river with no obvious visual classic chub swims will
open up new areas of river to explore, areas that you walked past on your
way to that textbook raft three-quarters of a mile away.

The silt bed connection has been the most important lesson of my winter
chub fishing; strange that it took a clout on the back of the head from an
Arlesey bomb to bring it in to focus. Like Jimmy Greaves says on the
television, 'Funny old game 'innit?'

The Big River Approach

John Bailey

The first three days had been spent on the Wye's tributaries, which to us made sense considering the giant I lost in the New Year period on a smaller stream. Furthermore, the main river had been fluctuating wildly and clarity had been low, with a lot of dirty water. In the summer, the river runs generally clear and the fish are highly visible. Stalking is quite possible and the intimacy of the approach makes the river seem less large and more accessible. In winter, this advantage is of course lost and the Wye appears truly what it is — a fast, wide river of immense power and body. Yet big rivers need not always demand specialised methods. Indeed the often wooded banks of the Wye are perfect territory for the wandering approach. Every alder bush, every raft, each eddy and slack, every glide and any undercut will, it seems, hold chub. Travelling light, flicking baits into each feature and moving on again is a sure way to take a haul of fish on the Wye, and on several other big rivers. The Severn is a further example of a water where the rear side is packed with chub clinging to any salient feature.

The Wye also has its confluences and it was on one of these that we settled on the fourth day. The pool created by the two flows of water was very deep and 'sinewy', sometimes heavy and boiling as a muscle of water flexed and bulged. This was in the eye of the confluence, and quickly beneath that the Wye ironed herself out into a slow, steadier pace; it was in this flow that we elected to fish. Miller settled rather upstream, casting into the tail of the confluence and letting his bait trundle down to where the river shallowed before pushing off down the glide. His line was 5lb BS straight through to the hook. Bait was flake or meat, both used large on a size 6 hook. Two SSG shot a foot up the line were his starter weights, which he added to or took off in frequent experiment.

Twenty yards beneath him I decided to give the feeder a trial. I used a large one that was open-ended, packed with mashed, flavoured bread just firm enough to stay inside when cast and get down the seven to eight feet to the riverbed before breaking up. Hookbaits varied between flake, again, and giant lobworm, both fished on the same size 6. My quivertip nodded, red and white, against a backdrop of dour, mid-Wales hills.

Miller was in at once, first cast I believe.

Miller was in at once, first cast I believe. The bait had rolled barely five yards when from the corner of my eye I saw him strike and then I heard him call. For nearly a minute in that rush of water we half-believed a barbel was on the end by the way it hugged the bottom and made off with rapid, powerful thrusts. But no; it was a chub . . . a typically splendid Wye three-pounder; deep, gold, unblemished, and vibrant in the hand. We returned it at once so that it could stay that way. Miller took three more such chub whilst I sat without a decent bite to strike at. Trembles on the tip made me believe that fish were present but just not having the hookbait as they should. The mobility of Miller's rig held the key and when I swapped the large feeder rig for a lighter one I was quickly into my first fish of the session.

It does not do to underestimate big river chub. Men like Ron Lees and Archie Braddock on the Trent have made a real study of them and I remember days fishing alongside them with real affection. Ron is an ace with a stick float, neatly and delicately shotted, light line, tiny hook and caster for bait. He fishes tight inside, inching the bait down the swim and fooling fish that were veterans of many a match day. Archie pursues perhaps even more wary fish on the ceaselessly hammered Trent. There he excels with the feeder, but not in my crude, amateurish fashion. I remember him showing me the baits he took for a single session three or four years ago; maggots, corn, worms, cheese pastes, meat pastes, seeds of all sorts, and everything carefully dyed and flavoured to place it apart from the norm. His feeders were home-made and perfectly adapted to his rivers. His rods were specially built. All in all he went to work in the most measured, thoughtful way and all day long the chub obliged him. I, on the other hand, had just one tiny barbel!

Another very worthy Trent chub angler is Frank Barlow; both have made valuable contributions to this book concerning big river chub fishing. Read on!

Chub on the Trent:
Now and Then

Frank Barlow

A cult figure to both J.B. and R.M., who eagerly awaited his weekly column in the *Anglers' Mail*, Frank has contributed a very important piece to this book in that he has described his relationship with the River Trent over the last thirty or so years. Its ups and downs are a stark reminder to all chub anglers just how fragile the habitat of chub is and how it can remain threatened even after a nationally applauded 'clean up' campaign has been seen to work.

The former editor of *Coarse Fisherman* magazine, which has Frank to thank for helping to bring it out of the doldrums and securing its place as an important monthly magazine again. Frank has considerable respect in the angling world, but it is his match fishing successes that have made him a household name in that sphere. He is a modest man who will be embarrassed at the mention of a fraction of his winnings; namely the holder of the Derbyshire Derwent match record, winner of the 1985 Chesterfield Open with his best-ever match weight being 105lb 9oz of Trent chub.

Frank has the considerable distinction of being indirectly responsible for the singularly most hilarious event ever witnessed by J.B. A full-sized cardboard cut-out of Frank was at a *Coarse Fisherman* stand at a certain tackle show in 1989, the cut-out supporting the canopy under which the 'team' were working. J.B. there witnessed a poor soul spending at least two minutes talking about chub fishing on the River Trent to the cut-out – Frank having slipped away for a swift pint of best! After a puzzled stare into the cut-out's face a rather sheepish punter sidled out of the hall never to be seen again. What was doubly amusing was that the life-size photograph was in black and white. Frank could never be described as pale and lacking in colour!

A very cold and bleak November day, way back in 1955, found me fishing with my father on the River Trent just above the suspension bridge on the

A 'live' Frank Barlow and nearly twenty-six pounds of chub.

'steps'. This is the part of the Trent that passes right through my native Nottingham. There were quite a few anglers about that day as the river had shown the first signs of recovery after the terrible cyanide pollution it had suffered three years earlier. Roach had arrived all along this section as if from nowhere, and they were very obliging too! Double-figure nets of fish ranging from two ounces to ten ounces were there for the taking. I did not find it so easy, however. I had been fishing for only a year or so; football, cricket and just about anything possible on grass had always been my preference. My dad, who was a very good national angler, saw his chance to get me hooked on fishing, so to speak. He had taken a fair bag of fish in a couple of hours, and had decided to pack up and come to sit with me. Here was where my serious angling career was to start, with an in-depth lesson from the old fellow.

He shotted me up a proper rig, explained the importance of the 'business end' of the tackle, and before long I was hooking a roach almost every trot down. The next step was getting them out of the water properly. His words I remember as if it was only yesterday – 'Feel the fish through the rod, pull steadily and "bat" the reel to take up the line.'

Things went very well for an hour or so, then something entirely different happened. I hooked a fish, but could not get the thing to come towards me. 'Come on son, remember what I've told you,' Dad said, thinking it was just another roach. He sat there wondering why I had faltered, but all was soon revealed as a pair of oval-shaped white lips appeared. 'You've got a chub!' he shouted. I had heard of these fish but had never seen one; we were both very excited as it lay there in the landing net. Anglers from close by came up to look at it and I felt very proud – of myself, but of my dad most of all. A pair of 'little samsons' were produced and the needle went down to 1lb 8oz. I well remember Dad and his mates saying that the river must really be getting cleaner now if chub were beginning to show again. At the end of the session I returned my fish but I could not resist another little hold of the welcome stranger. As I did, admiring the sleek shape, a love affair began between the species and myself, one which is still with me as I write, for they have given me so many hours enjoyment on all sorts of waters, in all sorts of conditions. Had I not become a dedicated matchman, I am sure my leisure time would have been taken up in pursuit of this, my favourite of all fish.

I had to wait a full two and a half years before the capture of my next chub. I will never forget this one either; it weighed 1lb 10¼oz and helped me win my first-ever match. This was on the upper River Witham. A couple of years after that I started to fish the occasional open match, and in the early 1960s I used to visit the River Severn, in the Bewdley and Stourport

92

area. It was all chub and roach in those days and it was here I was subjected to several next-peg hammerings with bags of chub. I used to catch my quota but I could never get the quality fish that Messrs Bailey (no relation to J.B.) and Lewis seemed to catch on most matches. It took me far too long a time to discover eventually that they were catching their chub on humble bread. To try to get the method right, a colleague and I arranged a few pleasure trips to the area – armed with plenty of loaves we caught quite a few 2lb and 3lb-plus fish.

In fact we got quite good at it, and simply could not wait for the next match on the stretch to come round. Tragically, after that the river always seemed to be in flood and we could never give it a proper chance. Eventually the chub seemed to die off a bit in the area; the barbel were making more and more of a show and they, of course, required totally different tactics.

We left the Severn scene, and concentrated nearer to home. At that time I fished a match on the River Nene at Milton Ferry, and on following the scales saw the odd decent chub had been caught. I found this very exciting – it would give me the chance to give them the Severn treatment! Several visits

He asked if I would mind if he cast his plug towards the
bridge buttress.

were made to this lovely stretch of water and the chub were always obliging, they were real suckers for the bread flake, fished beneath a 'Topper Haskins' Avon float trotted down the middle of the river. Every visit would see my best fish improve, until one cold Saturday morning I thought I had got the daddy of them all. A beautiful chub, fin-perfect, which weighed 5lb 4oz. I felt true elation at that moment. I already had six chub around the 2½ lb mark in the net, but this was the one I wanted. What a pity it was not a match, I thought. Just then a pike angler appeared from under the railway bridge; he was casting and retrieving what looked like a small plug. We exchanged pleasantries and enquired of each other's catches. He asked if I would mind if he cast his plug towards the bridge buttress as sometimes big pike lurked there. I said by all means, I had had my enjoyment and was not bothered if I did not catch anything else. After half a dozen casts he was suddenly into one, not very big he said, but fighting well. The fish, though, was quicky netted and he shouted over that it was a chub, of all things. Scales were produced and soon he shouted across to me, 'Not bad, just over six.' I nearly fell off my box! I was sure my match-style tactics had been the downfall of my five-pounder, and here was one of the 'tow rope' brigade nonchalantly returning the biggest chub I was ever likely to see. He then told me that he had had a few like that from the same stretch. As he carried on walking up the bank I just stared at him in awe. That was a session I would never forget. There are to this day big chub in that stretch of the River Nene and I am convinced that the new record chub lives there. Unfortunately I never seem to get there these days except for the odd match, but perhaps one day such a chub will be mine . . .

From then on my chub fishing exploits took a back seat for a while as the roach fishing on my local River Trent became irresistible to me. I spent a lot of time practising, and was soon winning quite a few matches as a result. Roach had become my first love, for I ate, slept and dreamed them. The matches I entered at that time seemed a formality to me; turn up, fish, collect your winnings and go home. It's rather a different scene these days, with the luck of the draw playing an ever-increasing role in matches.

I recall some time in the late 1960s drawing a peg at Fiskerton in the Trent Championships. There were 1,596 anglers there that day, so a good draw was a must for any chance of success. Where my peg would be on the day was anyone's guess, but I was overjoyed to find it was the first one off the gravel and running on to the barge moorings. Usually a bad draw, on that day the old river was well coloured with a nice bit of slack water close in, so I felt more confident. I fished a small stick float in the slack and for the first two hours caught small roach and gudgeon on single caster. That was the 'in' bait at the time; even on that day it was casters or bust! After about three hours I had about 5lb of fish in the net and then the peg went dead. With the river only two feet deep there was little else I could try, so I stuck at it. Suddenly I was attached to what I thought was the bottom, but in the time-honoured cliché – the earth moved! To my delight, a few minutes later there was a very welcome chub of 2lb in my net.

I could not believe it, as to my knowledge there were no chub in the Trent at the time, except for the occasional one below the weirs. When I had another fish of the same weight shortly afterwards I thought I was dreaming. I proudly brought my fish out at the end of the match and the onlookers were as amazed as I was. The needle went round to 9lb 14oz, which was good enough to get me third place on the day and a very large lump of cash. They were the first Trent chub I had caught since that day on the steps with my dad some twelve years earlier.

Thanks to the old Trent River Board, the early 1970s found us with a much cleaner river, and chub and all sorts of 'alien' species of fish began to appear. Carp, bream, perch, dace and even the odd trout and salmon began to grace the river, but it was the chub that myself and my fellow matchmen realised you had to have in your net to stand any chance of winning matches.

The methods for catching them were just the same as for roach – stick float or waggler! The biggest change was the amount of bait used, as by this time the Leeds angler Dave Thomas and his colleagues had 'weaned' the fish on to bronze maggots and the chub seemed to prefer them to anything else. Their match wins had been incredible, but soon everyone was at it, with casters suddenly taking a back seat. So it then became anything up to a gallon of bronze maggots for a five-hour match; it was certainly different from 2½ pints of casters which would sometimes last you all weekend! Soon chub were turning up everywhere, the river seemed full of them and every well-known match venue was paying out regularly to me. I really took to this new style as I felt that you were always in with a chance. In the days when it was all roach you usually had to bring your swim on gradually and nurse it along, and if you were in contention, say, with one and a half hours to go, it was very rare that you could pull back any deficit. But this was not so with chub; with an hour to go and very little in the net you could still win, as I did many times. Constant but accurate feeding always was the downfall of many a chub. Until the swimfeeder burst on to the scene not many people realised just how important accurate and regulated feeding had to be. The swimfeeder proved it beyond all doubt – what better than your hookbait just behind your loose offerings? Fish took to this method in a way you

A stickfloat caught chub for John Wilson.

would not believe, and for a long time 90 per cent of all Trent matches were won on the feeder with chub.

I could not believe it at the time: all those lessons from my dad, tips picked up from some of the country's best anglers – surely it could not all be wasted? Instant chub fishing match anglers were being born. It was easy for them – go to the shop, buy a feeder rod and a few 'plastic pigs', chuck them out into the middle of the river and start hauling out fish. Many top-name anglers refused to do it. In fact I could mention half a dozen household names in the sport who put their rods away never to be seen again. But me being me, I soldiered on! I have won a bit of coin on the feeder here and there, but there is nothing to compare in my book with watching a float go through the swim nicely and cleanly. The feeder era boomed, as I have said, but it seems everything has its peak and now, on most venues, it is just another method. It has its good days, in fact it has its unbeatable days, but mostly now it's the old float methods that are winning again, and the chub that are still there have got a bit wary of the almighty splash that those 'plastic pigs' make every few minutes.

In the late 1980s it seems that the Trent is undergoing a real change as far as chub are concerned. I will not go into the reasons for this fully as I have discussed it in a number of publications. All I will say is that in far-off days when I caught that solitary fish on the steps, the river was mucky. We had the years when it was clean and it was full of chub. Now they are dwindling away again. (Without wishing to be political it seems that the new technical revolution of the 1980s has coincided with the demise of the Trent just as the industrial revolution coincided with its total demise at the turn of the century – J.B. and R.M.).

The upper reaches of the Trent, around Trent Lock, only produce specimen chub now, whereas fish in the 12oz to 2½lb bracket used to be commonplace; 3½ to 4lb chub are now the norm but the trouble is that they are very scarce. What has happened to that large population? Coming downstream to Long Eaton, chub are extremely scarce, yet around 1985 you could return a stone of fish knowing it simply would not be enough to win even a section prize. It's the same at Clifton; would you believe that in 1986 three-hour night matches would be won with 30lb-plus of chub. These same pegs only produce the occasional fish today. In and around Nottingham it does not appear to be as bad; there are still quite a few chub of all sizes. In fact, my son Dean took a 4¼-pounder in perfect condition off the steps only recently. The general trend, though, is depressing and if the chub were to disappear altogether no one would feel their loss more than me.

The main difference is that a couple of years ago I could simply go to the river and fish for chub. A guaranteed bag was possible – now it is not! When the chub do turn up, though, either in match or pleasure sessions, I get that old feeling, pretty similar to the one I had when I gazed down on my first-ever chub in the presence of the old gentleman all those years ago. Please God, never let them take it away from me.

A Day on the Wye

Roger Miller

It was at a point on the Wye which I cannot honestly say was in the domain of either England or Wales that I once again found chub fishing with a vengeance. Years had passed and I had moved on to other things, keen to experience as much of angling as possible. Chub had, I am sorry to say, represented my early days and I had pretentiously abandoned them in my passionate hunger for other species, most notably the gentle giants – roach.

I had first walked the stretch with the infamous 'Reel Screamer', England's most eloquent and esoteric bachelor, and together we were lost in the enchantment of the twisting, pulsating, muscular energy that lay before us, which some people describe as the middle Wye. I had simply seen nothing like it and, as we looked on, a salmon of no less than 25lb crashed out in front of us from a slow, deep glide that I was considering for the evening session. I realised that this river was not remotely like the Waveney or the Wensum, and that to fish the Wye successfully would be a river angler's greatest challenge. Me? I was simply intimidated by the place.

The trouble with walking the Wye is that the whole river is one chub swim, and you find yourself stopping and simply drooling over a dream chub swim only to walk fifty yards or so to find another even better. On and on we walked. Late October had seen the last of the salmon anglers and, as if to mock their passing, great salmon persisted in jumping clear of the river wherever we looked – great, dark, stale fish of between 20 and 40lb were not the kind of distraction I had been used to before! I eventually decided on a swim that was so obviously full of fish, so ridiculously exaggerated in its features, that I would openly defy any chub angler to walk past it without stopping to fish it.

It was an eddy of great size. The water there was still and it was possible to bobbin fish with the lightest bobbin I had in my bag. The bank was a sandy cliff-face type which plummeted down to the water's edge. A knoll from which to fish was ideally placed and I shall never forget the astounding pace and power of the main current that scraped the side of the stillwater of the eddy, causing the most pronounced crease in the flow I had ever seen. The colour of the eddy was slightly lighter than that of the main flow, and

It was at a point on the Wye – in England or Wales (I cannot honestly say which) – that I found chub fishing again with a vengeance.

We were lost in enchantment for the twisting, pulsating, muscular energy which lay before us.

This river was not remotely like the Waveney or the Wensum.

with two huge overhanging alder trees the pool, with its depth of fifteen feet or more, looked as good a swim as I have ever seen.

An hour passed as I sat hovering over the bobbin, which occasionally flickered as something brushed along the 4lb test line. I was perplexed; the 'dream' swim was anything but that. The deep crease in the water where the main flow roared by was beginning to draw my attention more and more. My logic was simple; I gradually began to suspect that the chub were tight up against the wall of fast water. I imagined myself as a chub and surmised that all I would have to do was sit on the bottom and occasionally dash out into the main flow to grab whatever looked appetising. I also believed that the area of slack water acted as a buffer to food, and whatever the river carried down its course would bounce along the crease and away.

A lump of flake was flicked slightly into the main flow, and with no lead it bounced its way downstream. Currents, cross-currents and wild vortexes pulled and plucked at the line but I was left in no doubt whatsoever that a chub had suddenly whacked into the bait. A bite almost barbelesque in its savagery preceded a fight conducted almost solely in mid-river; if you have ever played a 4lb Wye chub against the flow of one of the river's faster stretches you will know exactly what power to expect. To those who have not I can only say, go to Wales, for you will not be able to feel such splendid excitement in playing a chub thus anywhere else in Great Britain.

It never ceases to amaze me how game-like coarse fish are from essentially game rivers; slim, vibrantly muscular, incredibly strong fighters and perfect in every scale and fin. It is easy for game anglers to believe that their precious game fish are 'superior' to their 'coarse' cousins, but, no, it is simply a question of habitat. Chub have to be these slim, fit beasts just to survive in the Wye, as do the roach, perch and dace. I am sure that a Wensum roach is not physically capable of existing in the Wye simply because it is not adapted to do so; no more so in fact than the stillwater roach that are occasionally pumped into the upper Bure and Wensum. It is wrong to believe that a fish which has never had to sit in any sort of flow in its life will suddenly be capable of doing so in a fast-flowing river. This, I believe, is the reason why a chub in the Wye will fight harder, longer and more passionately than many other fish from slower-moving streams – they are simply fitter; they have no choice, they have to be in order to survive and not end up in the Severn estuary. Eventually the athlete was landed. It had done itself proud – it was exhausted, beaten, and had succumbed to its fate. Never had I experienced such simple respect for a fish as that Wye chub; what a beast. More beasts followed that day as I threaded the freelined flake down that crease – no, gash – in the water.

Currents, cross-currents and wild vortexes pulled and plucked at the line.

I was left in no doubt whatsoever that a chub had suddenly whacked into the bait.

A fight conducted almost solely in mid-river.

Eventually, the athlete was landed.

Slim, vibrantly muscular, incredibly strong fighters and perfect in every scale and fin.

Soon 'Reel Screamer' appeared over the knoll and proudly acclaimed his first Wye chub; it was with light hearts and jaunty strides that we yomped back to the hotel, anticipating the evening ahead, an evening of chub fights being remembered as we gazed into the open fire, an evening of inspired story telling as we gradually convinced ourselves that the very next day would see the capture of a true Wye 'lunker'. This is the Wye, my friend, and if it ever calls you, go, for there is no chub fishing anywhere in Britain quite like it.

My Approach to Big River Chub

Archie Braddock

Archie Braddock is the modern master within the Trent school of anglers that dates back to J.W. Martin (Trent Otter), Henry Coxon and even F.W.K. Wallis. His inventiveness and dedication in all fields of angling are so immense that he fully deserves this accolade.

EARLY DAYS AND WAYS

More than thirty-five years ago I fished the Trent regularly, catching the roach and gudgeon with which the river teemed, even though the water was heavily polluted at the time. To a schoolboy limited to bicycle range such a fish as the chub remained an exotic dream, unattainable. Imagine my excitement when I actually caught one, all four inches of it! Still, it must have parents, I reasoned, and I spent long hours, summer and winter, legering lobworms and cheese; but all they ever produced was roach, albeit of a better than average size.

In later years I graduated to a small motorbike, and eventually to a large 100mph-plus machine, which opened up all sorts of new venues. My first real chubbing took place on the Nutbrook stream, near Ilkeston in Derbyshire which was quite easy to jump across in places, overgrown, yet suddenly opening out into areas holding broken-down old locks (it was originally dug to carry coal barges from the nearby workings). It was an absolutely perfect place to learn stalking techniques, and it was here that I had my first chance to get within a few feet of a chub, flick a worm on its nose, and watch the actual take. Size? I think my best-ever fish from there was 2lb 5oz, but my memories of the chub I caught there by creeping and crawling around will remain long after bigger fish have been forgotten.

I moved on, this time to the upper River Witham near Newark. Shallow and clear, it was ideal for chub spotting, but with its steep flood banks the fish could also see me. So it was a case of camouflaged clothing, polaroids, and once more creeping into position. It was here that I first learned the value of trotted baits. Often, a bait cast near a fish would alarm it, yet from the high banks it was possible to see them lazily swing across the current to intercept the large pieces of flake I sent down to them under a float set just 2ft 6in deep. I caught bigger fish too, mostly over two pounds, and the occasional three. Cheese, worm, crust and flake were the baits in those days; even luncheon meat was still in the future. Trotting is grossly underrated by most chub anglers, even the specialist.

Becoming more ambitious, I moved to the upper Welland which was then, and still is, a fishery holding some really big chub. Slower and deeper than the Witham, with lots of weed and rushes, it proved much harder, only giving up its chub in return for real effort. Trotting and legering brought fish, with a gratifying number of threes, and I developed a good technique for the better fish. Working from swim to swim during the day I often spotted chub I couldn't catch. The swims were lightly baited with mashed bread, and left until later. When I returned I always made sure I approached from downstream. A piece of crust was the bait, with one swan-shot pinched on the line 2in from the hook. This was carefully cast upstream into the swim, the rod set with tip high in the air, and the bow of slack line watched. A take caused this line to drop slack quite dramatically and the bites were hardly ever missed. This is a well-proven method nowadays of course, but not often used.

My bread fishing for chub reached its peak when I moved on to the Derbyshire Dove. Winter days on the river saw me arriving at dawn to engage in a day's bread fishing. Two carrier-bags of mashed bread allowed me to feed each swim as I fished it over a mile or more of river. Some of this bread went way downstream in the flow, baiting up the lower swims in advance. By the time I reached the bottom of the stretch my last swim had probably had bread trickling through it for six to seven hours. Coinciding with the fading light, that last hour could be fast and furious, and often produced the best fish of the day, sometimes a four-pounder. I occasionally still have this sort of day on the Derbyshire Dove or Derwent. Thinking of the Derwent brings to mind January to March 1963, the big freeze. All the lakes were frozen solid, as was the Witham and Welland, and only the fast-flowing Derwent near Derby was ice-free. So I spent that terrible winter actually trotting flake with a centre-pin, and caught good chub even with iced-up margins and icebergs floating downriver. I only failed once, and on that day the air temperature never rose above 15°F *below* freezing. I just couldn't get the bait on the hook as the moisture in the bread itself froze.

So in 1973 I returned to the Trent, originally for barbel, but finding so many chub it was unbelievable. Where nearly twenty years before I had searched hard for Trent chub, now they were swarming everywhere; in fact it was very difficult to avoid them, and I covered swims spread over seventy-odd miles of river. During the ten years from 1973 to 1983 I experienced some of the best chub sport it was possible to have, taking thousands of fish by a wide variety of methods.

My first approach was simple legered cheese, with the rod propped up at a steep angle as I watched the tip for bites. No problems here; the rod usually whacked round a foot or more, half the fish hooking themselves. I tried several different areas, and it soon became apparent that the chub were bigger the lower downriver I went. In the higher reaches towards Burton on Trent the fish swarmed, literally one per cast, but most of them were around 1lb. Lower down, Nottingham to Newark, and down into the tidal water, the fish averaged over 2lb, though were not quite so numerous. The first time I fished the Newark Dyke stretch, I picked a spot where the river narrowed and went very fast, and I legered a big knob of cheese on a no. 6 hook and 6lb line. As is usual, it was fairly quiet until sunset, then the river came alive. I experienced a succession of rod-wrenching bites, taking fourteen chub between 2½ and 3lb in an hour and a half. My arms were nearly dropping off after the slogging battles in the fast currents.

Another classic bait was luncheon meat. In the 1970s I used to buy this in 4lb tins, dozens at a time! I tried two baiting-up sessions. One was on the upper reaches, where I put in 8lb of meat the evening before I fished. From the first cast to the last, more than four hours in total, I caught a monotonous run of chub, all about 1¼lb each, before I got fed up with it. Next time out I baited a swim lower downstream, looking for barbel. Hopefully, to 'feed off' the chub, I put in 20lb of meat the previous evening; a mammoth task in itself, cutting that lot into bait-sized cubes. No barbel showed, but the chub went barmy; twenty-nine fish over 2lb, plus an 8lb carp. Once again I ended the session shattered. Incidentally, I once watched one of our local matchmen using luncheon meat, and he diced it really fine. Trotting tiny bits on a 16 hook under a stick float, and feeding handfuls as if they were maggots, he caught a huge number of 4 to 8oz chub, easily beating the maggot and caster men around him.

One very interesting fact about Trent chub is their willingness to feed in the dark, even in winter. For the hardy soul it means no loss of evening fishing; when the clocks are changed you just carry on! A really pleasant way to fish is laying on with float tackle and maggots, with a betalight fitted to the float. I find a bankside slack, get set up well before dark, and put in some groundbait and maggots around the float. If there's some colour in the water, bread flake can be an excellent change bait. The anglers going home in the falling light may complain that the fishing is dead, and so it would seem until about half an hour into darkness. Then the bites start, and by regularly feeding the swim with bait and groundbait it's possible to keep the chub going all night. No, I've never stayed all night in January or February, but I have stuck it until 1.30 a.m. and never stopped catching. Six or seven hours of non-stop sport is more than enough for me, not to mention the fact that even I feel the cold sometimes.

SPINNING

Then I turned to light spinning, and what a revelation that was. Trent chub are hugely predatory and take artificials freely, an added advantage being that they will hit lures in bright sunlight when all other methods and baits can be a bit of a struggle. Some of my best days with Trent chub have been spent with a small back-pack, a rod in one hand and a landing net in the other. Roving along the river, casting here and there, taught me a great deal about where chub lived and where they didn't. My tackle was a 9-foot carbon rod, small fixed-spool reel and 6lb line. I always used a short wire trace, as it made no difference to the chub, and made sure I didn't leave a spinner fast in a pike's mouth. Probably my most successful lure was a gold Mepps no. 2, going up a size or two for longer casts. I also found there were odd days when only a black lure would catch, in spite of going through every colour I had. Veltic and Ondex are other good makes, but everything is worth a try. No special movement was needed, just a steady retrieve.

It was noticeable that the chub tended to group together in small areas on some days, with perhaps a quarter of a mile of river producing the occasional small fish, then suddenly it's one after another. One spot gave me thirteen fish in the first fourteen casts, and a total of twenty-six in one and a half hours, before the swim died. Obviously such areas received more visits with bottom-fishing tackle, once located. My best spinning session to date gave me fifty-six fish in four hours one August afternoon, of which six were pike and three were perch, so lure fishing for chub can be an extremely successful method.

I've done some float fishing on the Trent, stick float trotting for roach, which has produced many chub, and the most interesting thing has been the effect of flavours added to the maggots. I have been doing some experimenting with this, and my impression has been that chub really like the spicier flavours, like curry, in cold winter water. Having said that, I also did well with cheese flavour, and told *Coarse Angler* editor Colin Dyson about it. He tried cheese-flavoured maggots on his tidal section, and immediately caught some big chub and roach. Unfortunately he didn't take his scales, but he's adamant that the chub exceeded 5lb, and the roach topped 2lb! There is obviously room for experiment here, as there is with boilies. Several carp anglers I know have been inundated with chub whilst using fish-flavoured boilies, with odd fish topping 4 and 5lb.

FEEDERS

Many anglers, matchmen in particular, like feeder-fishing chub, and this is one area where I've spent a great deal of effort, and still do. With so many chub about, I decided to use big feeders and really put down a good carpet of feed every cast. In a four- or five-hour evening session I could build the swim up by sheer volume of food available. After all, my luncheon meat bait-ups had shown it was impossible to overdo it. I soon found that commercially made feeders wouldn't take the pounding of continuous casts into mid-river, literally disintegrating during the first session. Eventually I made my own by sawing up the aluminium suction tubes on vacuum cleaners, drilling holes, and glueing lead to them.

I always use open-ended feeders, as I feel that the groundbait plugs in each end are an essential part of the approach. To make the groundbait I use two parts brown crumb to one part bran. The bran ensures the mix cannot clog, which is vital, as the idea is to deposit a good handful of seeds on the river bed. Seeds? Yes, I believe scores of little items will hold the fish there, searching around, and there are several which will do the job. Hemp is the obvious first choice, but sweetcorn, maize and wheat have all worked well for me. I feel that many others may do the business, perhaps chick peas, black eye beans, maple peas, and how about diced luncheon meat, or mini-boilies, or even elderberries? There's a lot to be tried and I'm sure most of them will work. Even maggots and casters still catch, although they have been hammered hard by the thousands of matchmen. I soak my seeds in water first, to which I may add one of the commercial liquid flavours. The same flavour is also added to the water which is used to dampen the groundbait plugs, the idea being to send a tell-tale 'taste' flowing down the current. If the bait is also soaked or dipped in the same flavour then you've done everything possible to enhance your presentation. What flavours? I'm not giving everything away, but try any of the fishy or cheesy ones.

There have been many different end rigs suitable for feeder fishing described in the angling press, some involving one or more loops in the line. Having gone very deeply into this, trying many varieties, I now use one or two very simple layouts. The diagram is self-explanatory, i.e. a fixed paternoster. Any form of sliding rig *doesn't* slide unless you fish at very short range with virtually no flow. The 6in feeder link allows a total movement of about twelve inches, which means the tip has gone round a long way. A 'smash and grab' take hits the feeder, turning the set-up into a self-hooking rig. When using a heavy bait like cheese or luncheon meat I put a swivel in at the junction, and if it's tied as in the diagram the weight of the feeder forces it to stand out, like a 'boom'. With light baits like corn, casters, and so on I use a small brass ring which can be bought from specialist angling suppliers.

BAITS

As far as baits are concerned, two have done extremely well for me. Cheese/ crust special is just that, a piece of crust on the bend of a long-shanked hook, and cheese built up along the shank in a pyramid shape. My other special is sausage-meat mixed into a paste with crushed wheat flakes. Another approach is to use ordinary bread paste with 5ml of flavour mixed into the water used to make the paste. With a couple of hundred flavours on the market, plus possible mixes of any two or more, there's more than enough to keep the angler going for a lifetime.

For the man who wants the bigger chub only, dead fish are the answer. Back in the early 1970s I first tried deadbaiting for Trent pike, and immediately started getting lots of fast takes, which I missed. The first chub I caught weighed over 3½lb, and had taken a 6oz chunk of mackerel on a wire trace. Since then I've refined the method for chub fishing, but for a long time I had problem with missed takes. The crunch came in the winter of 1987 when I had nine positive bites in two hours, but caught only *one* 3lb chub. So I gave it a lot of thought and experimentation, and finally solved the problem. The trouble was, wherever you put the hook in the bait, the chub would grab the other end! Obviously a hook in each end of the dead fish was tried, but trebles were treated with caution, and singles tended to lie flat against the bait.

The solution was double hooks, Drennan back-to-backs, size 8. With one hook of each double buried firmly in the bait at each end, the remaining hook stands proud, giving the effect of fishing two singles. It's impossible

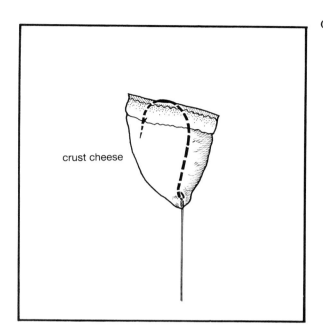

Cheese crust special.

crust cheese

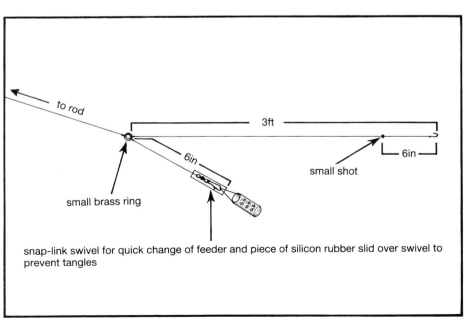

to rod

3ft

6in

small shot

6in

small brass ring

snap-link swivel for quick change of feeder and piece of silicon rubber slid over swivel to prevent tangles

The taking fish has 12in of free movement.

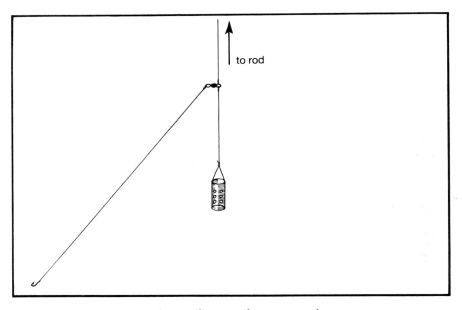

The weight of the feeder forces the swivel to act as a boom.

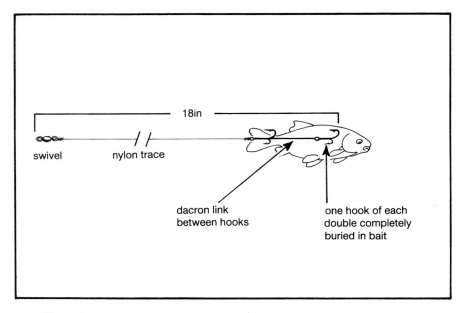

Deadbait rig.

for the chub to take the bait off, or get hold of it without coming into contact with a hook. I now hit nine out of ten takes. The line between the two hooks is soft Dacron, not because it's necessary for cautious fish, but to enable me to wind the Dacron easily around the bend of one of the hooks, thereby effectively shortening the link for different-sized baits.

Almost any fish, coarse or sea, works for bait, but as a general rule I find a dead gudgeon can be excellent in the summer, while sprat, sardine and mackerel (in 2 to 3oz chunks) work best in the winter. I usually cut fish up and sprinkle bits in while fishing, but if you can get down the day before and bait up with a couple of chopped-up herring or mackerel, the results can be greatly improved. I use two rods for deadbaiting. One is fished down the near-bank slack on a simple running leger rig, with an optonic for bite indication, the other is the usual fixed paternoster, fished further out in the flow on a quivertip. Winter, say from November onwards, is by far the best time, fishing from one hour before dark to two to three hours after.

I have detailed several different methods in this chapter, but I have not covered various others, like trotting big lobworms for example, simply because I have not yet done enough of it to be certain of positive results. That's the beauty of chub fishing; there's always something else to do. May it always be so.

The Stillwater Chub Approach

John Bailey

Llandrindod Wells was our target as the nearest place to replenish our rapidly dwindling supply of gear. If you set out to fish the Wye feeling you have enough bombs and hooks for a week, then frankly, you have just got to double the number! This great river rolls whole trees down from Wales when the floods push through, and in them live the best of the chub. Furthermore, over the centuries the force of the water has gouged out great shafts through the rock, and on the edges of the boulders the lines are cut and more tackle is lost. Fifteen, sometimes twenty breaks a day *each* was quite normal. It was soul-destroying, irritating and environmentally un-pleasant to have to fish like this, but what alternatives were there? We had to get down to the fish wherever their snaggy hideouts were and, thank God, it is our belief we did not actually lose any fish once hooked – just unattached gear. After well over a hundred bombs had been abandoned our stocks were down and all but out, and we were off a dozen miles or so to the tackle shop.

Llandrindod Wells is a strangely exotic place. It is an old spa town and therefore an unlikely-placed holiday resort. It possesses fine arcades, parks and grand buildings all beautifully and eccentrically out of place in the bosom of rural Wales. The town's tackle den is a similarly delightful type of place. The shop is welcoming and full of time, if you know what I mean: advice, interest and encouragement are all freely passed on there . . . the most excellent bombs, hooks and new lines. Our odd English desire for chub was treated considerately, with a degree of benign humour. We felt they almost understood how we could be wanting to catch something so lowly in the traditional Welsh kingdom of the salmon. After all, the gentleman tackle dealer does see a fair few coarse fishermen these days – especially so since the ornamental lake in the centre of the town has become ever more famous for its carp. The fact that our old friend Chris Yates caught his first-ever twenty from the water is enough to ensure many a

Roger Nudd with a 6lb 2oz stillwater Norfolk chub.

man's pilgrimage westward, and all of them must at some time make their way to the town's tackle shop for supplies.

It was our tackle dealer who now repeated a tale first told to us back in 1987. It concerned the infamous Quarry Pool that we had then visited along with Mr Yates and his friend Mr James. Certainly there were chub in there, the dealer assured us, transported up from the Wye and grown fat on the shoals of sticklebacks in the place. It would be well worth a visit, he felt, and after hearing about 'chub the size of carp' we could not but agree.

We found the correct road, which led us high up a hill overlooking the town. We parked and made off along a rough path, up towards the grey skies above. Our walk was not a long one, but it was steep and awkward and the weight of our gear made us stop a good few times before the final crest was reached. There, spreading beneath us, was a large, flat plateau and, at the far side, a scree dropping almost sheer into a hell's mouth of deep, dark water . . . the Quarry Pool!

Quite how to tackle the acre of water, we were not sure. Sticklebacks freckled the margins in hordes and seemed to be so contented and unharried we felt that the surface layers must probably be chubless in the daytime. We plumbed the pool here and there and found it extraordinarily deep, so deep in fact that neither of us fancied fishing on the bottom. But then, what was left to us? How on earth would a knob of bread or a lump of cheese look to any fish dangling absurdly in mid-water? It was then, with not a great deal of conviction, that we made a start. We cast two bottom baits to an area that seemed slightly shallower, with good rocky cover. The rods were placed on rests and optonics, and then we began to spin the rest of the pool with spoons and plugs. We kept at the task for some hours, varying lures, baits and positions, but the pit was dead. Our confidence, always dubious, sank even lower. Miller looked at me steadily, and with absolute finality stated, 'My rods are coming in!' And that was that!

I do not doubt that there are chub in the Quarry Pool. I am quite sure, too, that they have thrived there: river chub very frequently do when moved to still waters, where prey fish are plentiful. In Norfolk, two small pits stocked with Wensum and Bure chub have yielded 6lb fish to both John Wilson and Roger Nudd. And what chub they were! Massively deep and thick-bodied, with rich colouring and powerful-looking shoulders. I do not think either fish was particularly long, however. In all probability they were mature fish of some 4lb or so when they were moved and all this extra weight was made up of muscle and fattening out. The whole issue of stillwater chub is stirring. Peter Stone's huge 7lb fish fell from a pit and I remember hearing Andy Hughes tell me of a near-double figure chub from a well-known southern still water.

Perhaps, though, the most extraordinary stillwater chubbing saga is told by Phil Tew. After reading it, you will possibly say that it is the most gripping chub tale ever told . . .

A Night to Remember

Phil Tew

Phil Tew is one of the many superb but low-key specialist anglers within the dynamic and forward-thinking National Association of Specialist Anglers (NASA), which boasts members from all over the country. It is with the very kind permission of NASA, through one of its leaders, Dr Bruno Broughton, that permission has been granted to reproduce Phil Tew's article here – having originally been published in the magazine of NASA, *Specialist Angler*.

If anyone can remember back to the winter of 1981–82, they will recall the high winds, followed by the big freeze-up which put everyone out of action for several weeks. I, too, did not fish for three weeks, and spent my time moping around the house with nothing to do except gaze at the photographs of the 6lb 3oz chub I had caught just before the foul weather set in.

As I sat at home one night, my mind began to work on a new rig which I could use to put up my catch rate. I was thinking of a means of eliminating the feel of the wire trace when it came into contact with a big chub's lips, and I also wanted a way of attracting the fish. The idea I came up with may sound crude, but it worked – on the first occasion, too! I threaded several ⅜in-square pieces of foam rubber on to some trace wire, and then attached two size 10 trebles as normal. Not surprisingly, the wire trace could not be felt at all. The other part of the idea was to soak the foam in a mixture of pilchard oil, a fish essence, and coat it in dried ox blood. When this concoction lay on the bottom, it ought to give off a strong scent – attracting chub from a great distance.

All I waited for now was a chance to use it, and fortunately I did not have to wait long. On Thursday morning I telephoned the owner of the water, and he gave me the good news – the ice was thawing rapidly. I quickly 'crawled' round my boss for the last day's holiday he owed me, hoping he would let me take the next day as leave. He agreed and, after a long lay-off, I knew I would at last be fishing tomorrow.

Thursday afternoon dragged on and on; the suspense was killing me. I had such a feeling of confidence that I could not wait to get away. Five

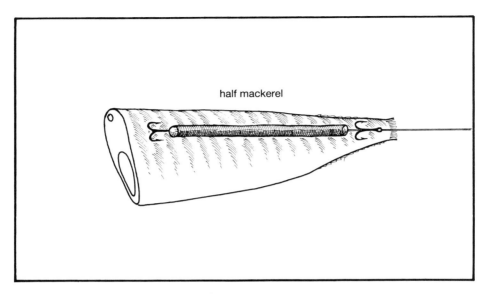

half mackerel

Trace with ¼in foam covering soaked in pilchard oil and
fish essence, then dipped in powdered ox blood.

o'clock eventually arrived when – no – bleep, bleep, my pager went off. I am a plumber and my company provides an emergency out-of-hours service. There was a burst water-main awaiting me in Kensington and I quickly made the dash from South Harrow. I completed the job in record time and arrived back in Kingsbury at 6.55 p.m. I decided that it was now too late to start fishing that night, but I would set off very early the next morning. The last thing I did before retiring was to pack my van in readiness for the next day.

I was on my way at 4 a.m., and the wind was very strong as I drove down the motorway. I turned the van heater up to full blast as it was still savagely cold. I arrived at the water at 5 a.m. and was relieved to see that there was not another soul in sight – I had the swim I wanted.

I decided to fish for pike during the day and managed a few fish into double figures. Just as it was getting dark I had a very fast run. I wound down and gently struck into nothing! On inspecting the bait I knew that it had been a chub, so I immediately changed over to the new rigs in conjunction with the bait I had been using – mackerel tail. Fifteen minutes later I landed a small jack of 4lb. Nothing else happened except that the wind became stronger still, blowing great billows of froth to where I was fishing. The indicators were continally being blown off, making my heart jump. In the end I even had to secure the rods in the rests to stop them being blown in too! I also experienced trouble from great rafts of weed which drifted across my lines and which had to be cleared periodically.

In normal circumstances I think I would have reeled in and got my head down. But I still had this feeling – a very strong feeling – that something was about to happen, so I persevered against the wind and the weed. Mind you, there was little I could do to stop either! Whilst eating my dinner I also had problems with the wild cat that lives there: it probably smelt my cooking, and scared the living daylights out of me when it jumped up on to the roof of my van. Later still, the rats came out, dragging away my bags of bait. Oh what a night! I think the indicators were, on average, pulled off every thirty minutes, and it was a tedious job resetting them in the dark. All I hoped for was that the wind would calm down a little, just enough to give me a break. It did not! I was still there, wide awake, at 3.30 a.m. and decided to stay awake all night. I continued to experience that eerie feeling that something was about to happen. As I sat in front of the van my eyes became very heavy, and I rested my head on the back of the seat. I must have dozed off as all I can remember was dreaming . . . I can see my rods . . . I can see the indicators tight up under the reels . . . I see the line tighten . . . the indicator falls off . . . I was woken by the buzzer going off. When I reached my rods, one of the Ron Pendleton-type indicators was off, the line was peeling rapidly from the spool. A gentle strike was made, and I was 'in'.

I knew it was a chub straight away by the familiar thump, thump on the rod tip. I then lost contact with the fish and had to wind down feverishly to discover whether or not it was still on. It was, and was coming towards me rapidly. I regained control. It cannot be far from the bank now. With the landing net at the ready, I started to pump the fish hard, and in she went at the first attempt. I bit through the line and carried the net up the bank. When I turned on my torch, I saw a staggering sight: there on the bank lay the biggest chub I have ever seen. Her length was 22½in, her girth was 15¾in and she weighed in at 7lb 1oz. The time was 5 a.m.

I slipped her gently into a keepnet as I had to find a witness, and hoped that someone would arrive at first light in preparation for a day's pike fishing. Believe it or not, the wind actually dropped a bit, so I cast out a fresh bait, lit a cigarette and drank a well-earned cup of tea. At 7 a.m. Peter Stone arrived and we took a few photographs of the fish. We checked the weight on his scales: sure enough, it was 7lb 1oz. Then, the fish was returned to the water to fight again another day. It truly was a fantastic fish, and to come in a dream . . . wonderful! Yes, it was certainly a night to remember.

The Monster Syndrome

John Bailey

Both Miller and myself are confused by the Wye and its supposed monsters. Why does there seem to be so few really large chub? Are most stories simply false? After all, out of a hundred or more chub caught over the last three years by us both, the best either of us have managed are low 'fives', with most running between 2 and 3lb. The lost monster of the New Year of 1989 has been the only occasion either of us has felt close to something really exceptional. Yet both of us know men along the river who claim to have caught or seen the calibre of chub we are after; but in all cases photographs have been lacking. We still believe them, however! Past experiences suggest that it is very difficult to know exactly what a chub river holds. Surprises can and do happen. Take, for example, my River Wissey lost fish which I once described in a 1970 article; that clonker was a real one-off amongst hordes of very moderate fish. A similar thing happened to me on the upper Yare, again in the 1970s . . .

THE TWO THAT GOT AWAY

Before the season closed I returned to a swim where ten years earlier I lost the greatest fish of my life. The swim is on the upper Yare, perhaps Norfolk's most underrated river. Back in the winter of 1976–77 I had taken roach and perch to 2lb or a little over from a number of different swims, and my confidence was growing. I had also had a surprise bream, and John Wilson had taken a 5lb chub a year or two earlier, so I knew almost anything could turn up.

On a Sunday afternoon, I settled into yet another new swim. It was a tight little bend with a good eddy and a textbook crease. The river here ran through a copse and alders hung over the far bend. The swim smacked of perfection and I was not at all surprised to get a bite first cast.

The fish felt heavy, but I quickly saw that it was a chub and I hustled it to the net. It looked fairly big, but I had my roach hat on and I did not consider it too carefully. I half-wondered whether to net it and wait for J.J., my

A superb Wensum brace – 5lb 7oz and 6lb 2oz.

partner, who had the scales, but I decided not to risk the disturbance, and took it a few yards upstream to turn it loose. Towards dusk, J.J. arrived at the swim and sat by me as darkness closed in. I had a second bite, and landed a second chub. This was considerably smaller than the first one, but as the scales were with me, this time it was weighed. That chub was an ounce under 5lb! That first fish had to have been 5½lb or more and I was a thoughtful, remorseful angler that night – it is not everyone who throws back his personal best chub so lightly! The sessions rolled by and all produced roach. I saw no more chub and they rather faded from my mind. Cold weather set in. Bites became tentative and then stopped altogether. I had to fish finer, and by dropping to 1.1lb bottoms and size 20 hooks I again picked up the roach.

The nights were pulling out sufficiently to allow me two or three hours on the river after work, and I was more than happy to brave the cold. The night in question, however, was not only cold, but windy too. I all but gave the river a miss, but finally decided on the swim in the copse where I could at least have some shelter from the beastly easterly. So on that fine, clear afternoon, I made my way over frost-rimed marshes. The sun was far down

A true monster chub – 6lb 2oz for Alan Rawden.

as I cast, yet within minutes I saw the slightest of bites on my quivertip and was straight into a fish. It surfaced at once in mid-stream and just strolled there for a minute against the current before it sounded.

It made every chub I had either caught or seen before look totally insignificant. This was a truly massive fish and I realised with immediate clarity the task that lay before me. To bring a chub nearer 7lb than 6 – or even bigger than that – to the bank on such a line and hook would demand something of a miracle. I set to it, though, as the sun fell towards the wooded horizon and I played that fish oh-so-gently that even when the wind rattled the line my heart froze.

For a long while I feared that such wand-like pressure could never tell on a fish and I was forced to follow the chub wherever it wished to go, both upstream and down. My fingers had quite frozen and my hope had all but gone when I began to sense the fish was swimming higher in the water. The runs were weakening, and at very long last his fins were as much out of the water as they were in it.

For the first time, the idea that I might land this fish seemed less laughable and more possible. The dying minutes of that battle on the Yare are painful to remember even now. Had I lost the fish at the very beginning, I would have cursed, but not despaired. Now I began to feel I had been granted some luck and that I had ridden it to the absolute limit of my ability. In that freezing sunset, I sensed that I deserved this mammoth chub. It was faltering, and nearly on its side. I began to reach for the net knowing I had only a rod's length to draw it in. The fish came close, very close. I saw the size 20 hook clinging to a sliver of skin. The last seconds – the net rim was in sight. The chub gave a last buck and on the light, tight line, just this was too much. I saw the fish now – righting, turning, dropping back to the depths away from me, as it turned out, forever.

I feel sure that Yare fish was a pioneer, a fish setting out to move into virgin territory to colonise it. These always seem to be the big chub. Presumably there is little competition for them and they grow quickly. As their numbers increase, the average size of the chub decreases – in common with most fish species. The rivers Wissey, Waveney and Wye are all rivers that have legendary chub of 6, 7 and 8lb, caught by assorted means years ago when the chub were just beginning to establish themselves in these river systems.

My own experience of this was founded most conclusively on the Wensum. During the early 1970s there were chub in the lower reaches, but very few upriver. As the species trickled upstream it seemed to be the biggest fish that pushed forward the species limits. There were always very few

The tiny upper Wensum, home of pioneering monsters.

chub and never enough to pursue specifically. They came, therefore, on roach tackle but were invariably close to 5lb and over. Today there are fish throughout the higher reaches, but these big ones are now very rare and fish of 3lb are the norm.

So the Yare, the Waveney, the Wissey, the Wye – take any of them today and a big chub is very likely to be an elderly fish and almost certain to be very cautious. My experience with Moby Dick from my book *Reflections from the Water's Edge* (*The Crowood Press*, 1987) bears some repetition here.

MOBY DICK

I saw him in July in a well-worn swim above Norwich, known to all who fish thereabouts. That first instant, I took him for a small-to-medium common carp, so great was his width and so large his scales. Only when he turned and rose up through the water did I see him for what he was – an immensely long, deep and broad chub. If ever my six-pounder was saying hello, it was him.

Apart from his size, the only strange thing about the fish was an ivory whiteness to his head and his left flank. I named him Moby Dick on account of both his hugeness and his colour. And, just as that famous whale led its hunter Captain Ahab a merry dance over the seven seas, so that chub was to torment me on the Wensum.

I soon learned that the fish was a hungry one, but that two problems stood in my way. First, he was one of a shoal of thirty lesser specimens. Second, he was clever, a mastermind of the underwater world. I came to learn that if ever a fish should prove capable of thought on a near-human

A monster chub – 5lb 10oz – for the extraordinarily gifted Alan Rawden.

level then that fish would be Moby. . . . But I am ahead of myself. Back we must go to the early days and retrace the steps of that hunt.

A great number of his companions, all as hungry as chub ever are, convinced me it was hopeless to fish blind or at night. Over three days a dozen chub up to three pounds proved that. No, Moby had to be stalked. A bait had to be put to him, precisely, individually, if I were to cheat his smaller neighbours. Fortunately the river was clear and I could see what I was doing. Also, there was plentiful cover to make use of, but there my advantages ended.

I soon found that Moby would leave the cover of his raft and inspect the first bait that was drifted to him. But once that first cast was refused then all further attempts – even with changed baits – were totally ignored. It was as if Moby knew that an angler had moved in and it would pay him to lie low, under his coverlet of green. Quite obviously my next step was to anchor a bait close to the raft rather than fish it on the move. This is how 95 per cent of Norfolk chub men fish, watching the quiver, and this, I am quite sure, our Moby knew. Certainly, any static bait left him totally unmoved. I might have legered a lump of rock for all the interest he paid me on the bottom.

A four-pounder appeared faster than a polaris.

So I came to realise that my first attempt with a moving bait had to be perfect in every way or for that session I could wave him goodbye, wish him good day and move downriver for a barbel. I began to concentrate on presenting a bait at the right depth, with the right speed of fall, at the same pace as the river and on hook and line that were as inconspicuous as possible. Away from the fish, I tried again and again with bait after bait. Sometimes I used a float and sometimes I freelined. All combinations of shot were tried until at last I began to feel happy that I had the best combination for that flow rate with both particles and bigger baits.

The next day I moved into the raft swim with my confidence high. A big bait was my opening approach – a huge scoop of bread flake moulded around a size 4 hook that would take in water and bounce the gravels under his nose. It trundled towards him. He cocked an eye, when, dammit, a four-pounder appeared faster than a Polaris, scoffed the lot and put an end to that opening campaign.

Next day, I returned with two pounds of corn and a different plan altogether. For an hour I fed in the loose grains until I turned the water before me into a mass of surging, heaving chub. The threes and fours I had fighting for feed by my bank. Moby kept under a raft opposite, coming out now and again when I put two or three yellow grains down his side. Everything was set: the smaller fish busy and lured away; Moby interested and all alone. I felt I was close.

I had changed from conventional line to Drennan double strength 6lb test. Perfect. A size 14 buried deep in a grain of corn, a no. 6 shot six inches up, and a tiny quill at 3 feet completed the outfit. Now I would have just the one chance. An underarm flick and the bait landed dead in line to knock at Moby's front door. I steered it to him. At four feet, the big chub saw the bait and stiffened. Two feet and he came into open water to watch. A foot now and he came up to intercept. Nine inches, a nose-length, and a confident swallow – and Moby was pulling my string like a sperm whale from the tropics.

I lost him. It was keep him from the raft or say goodbye. The line held. The knots took it, but the hook came back straight as a needle. Like the Moby of old, the chub flicked his tail and was gone.

LOST OPPORTUNITIES, NEW HORIZONS

The loss of that fish reinforced my dire luck with chub: the Yare fish, the Wissey fish, Moby and the Wye monster all bade me sad farewell and as I write, I sometimes really doubt if I will get my 'six' to crown literally dozens of 'fives' throughout my career. I have no doubt that I have lost four fish well over that weight and probably at least two were over 7lb. I suppose a mixture of bad luck, over-light gear and a dash of bad angling has led to this tale of woe.

There are times, however, when all the lost four do is to spur me on to greater lengths and when I theorise about big fish – the joy of every angler – it is often about chub. Obviously, I am still ever on the look-out for rivers, or sections of rivers, where pioneers could be present. The river need not be large. It could be a river recovering from pollution. Whatever, chub will be a rarity there, probably little more than a rumour that needs to be followed up.

I also feel it is possible to approach typical big chub rivers like the Wensum, the Avon or the Stour with anything but traditional methods. I am convinced that big fish will fall to smaller livebaits, fished perch-style; deadbaits have tremendous potential; night fishing is an important approach. I fancy the underfished still waters that get flooded, albeit very occasionally, by chub-holding rivers. The most inaccessible sections of

This tiny feeder stream holds exceptionally difficult chub, to impressive sizes. It is also full of fry.

river, in my experience, hold the biggest of the chub. The big fish tire of the hassle of the flogged stretches and the endless competition for bait, and drift away where they can be masters of their own lives. Fred Crouch, in his book *Understanding Barbel*, has noted the same type of behaviour in that bigger species.

Very big chub do, I believe, need a supply of small fish. I am sure this is how many of the real whoppers have grown large. Coarse fish will provide the prey on most rivers, but how about those rivers with vast populations of salmon and trout? I am thinking of rivers like the Eden and of course, inevitably, the Annan. I cannot deny that our attention has been attracted by that river lately. The rumours of excellent chub have intensified the more we have visited Scotland and before this book is published, we will have investigated. In fact, one of our younger friends, Christopher Shortis, has already done some work up there, and his chapter follows.

.

Dr Cameron's Ten-Pound Annan Chub

Christopher Shortis

An ex-pupil of J.B.; Christopher is fortunate enough to live within yards of some of the best chub fishing in England, namely the Wensum near Norwich. Christopher has, in spite of his young age, many years' chub fishing experience under his belt. Groomed by that master chubber Trefor West, Christopher represents the young breed of angler who will undoubtedly be a 'name' in the 1990s and beyond. Thirsty for success with chub, he travels to such diverse places as the Hampshire Avon and Scotland's River

Christopher Shortis and a summer chub of 4lb 10oz from the Wensum.

Annan in search of ever more specimens. Christopher's fascination with the Annan, and in particular with the former record chub held by Dr Cameron, has led him to do more research into that particular fish than the Record Fish Committee could ever imagine. His findings are most revealing, and we are pleased to have the chance to publish them here, in Christopher's first article.

Perhaps the most talked-of former record of all is Dr Cameron's alleged double-figure chub. Many well-respected anglers have through the years written of their belief that the fish never existed. Unfortunately these gentlemen were trying to disprove things that did not actually occur. Let me explain; if the true facts of the 'record' were known, these writers would, like me, believe that the fish was caught, that it was a chub and that it did in fact weigh at least ten pounds. To begin with, I will outline the circumstances of the capture.

DR CAMERON'S BIG DAY

One evening in late June 1955; Dr J.A. Cameron of Dumfries was fishing for sea trout on a stretch of the River Annan twelve miles from his home. He was fishing with a friend, Mr Smith, a male nurse from Lochmaben. Some time during the evening Dr Cameron hooked a fish which fought for quite a while, staying deep and making quite long runs. The fish suddenly tired and was landed, unhooked, and after a few choice words, was killed (do not forget that Dr Cameron was a game angler, and the Annan essentially a game fishing river).

They returned home later that evening and as neither of them had been carrying any scales it was only then they discovered how much the chub, for so it was, actually weighed. On the river bank they had estimated the fish to be 'about ten pounds' and they were not far out, as the scales registered 10lb 8oz!

Dr Cameron returned home and went to bed. The following morning he went on a planned holiday to Morayshire for two weeks. Mr Smith, however, decided out of curiosity, to look up the chub record, and he discovered that their fish had beaten it by two and a bit pounds! It was at that point that Mr Smith made a record claim on behalf of Dr Cameron. Neither Mr Smith nor Dr Cameron had made any plans for the fish; first, they had not realised the chub had been a record, and second, Mr Smith did not know the chub may be required for examination. He therefore kept it,

133

Trefor West returns some Scottish cat food.

until it began to get 'a bit high', when it was decided to give it to an elderly lady neighbour who kept a great many cats. It was these cats who finally disposed of the fish.

On holiday, Dr Cameron bought his usual Sunday papers and opened them to discover, to his astonishment, that he had been awarded the chub record, and not only that; he had won a fishing rod and £25, too!

TALL STORY, OR TRUE STORY?

Dr Cameron was fishing for sea trout, not salmon or brown trout as other less informed accounts have suggested. He was using a 6lb test hook-link and a bob fly tied on to a size 10 hook; not a bad combination for a big chub! This rig gives some idea of the strength of the fish. Many disbelievers, who claim the Annan only contains a few fish larger than 4lb and nothing over 10lb, have said that he could not possibly have caught such a fish from that river. This simply is not true; the stretch where Dr Cameron caught his fish contains many chub with a high average size. A lot are over 4lb, several are over 5lb and the occasional fish does exist over 6lb. Any larger? Who can say, but even today it is possible.

There is certainly no shortage of food in the Annan. It teems with salmon parr and trout fry, there is a huge population of crayfish, a good run of elvers and prolific weed in summer which contains hundreds of nymphs and flies; the chub will feed on all of these. Consider, also, what the chub has to compete with for all this food. The salmon and the sea trout are migratory fish and, whilst it is not strictly true that such fish do not feed in fresh water, they are hardly competition for the rich supply of food in the Annan. Other non-migratory species which share the Annan with the chub are small brown trout, dace and grayling, but none occur there in great numbers. It is my belief that the larger chub in the Annan fulfil the role of predator, and I feel sure that the parr and fry of game fish supplement their already very rich diet, enough to make the odd chub in the Annan very big indeed.

It has been suggested that Dr Cameron mistook the chub for another fish, but it is worth pointing out that he had inadvertently caught a number of chub from the Annan in the past, as one might expect. The scales on which the chub was weighed were notoriously inaccurate, as indeed Dr Cameron himself has said. 'Ounces out' is how he described them, so in fact the chub may not have weighed 10lb 8oz but 10lb 4oz, or even 10lb 12oz; I think it is fair to say, however, that the chub was almost certainly into double figures.

My personal experience of Annan chub is that they are indeed the 'fearfullest of fishes', as the splash of the smallest piece of bread sends them racing back to the deeps. I believe that a fly would in all probability be the best way to tempt an extremely cautious, outsized Annan chub, especially if fished in the half-light of the evening. When cast properly, a fly makes the minimum of disturbance and by its very definition it imitates natural food. I have seen many Annan chub ignore bread, probably because they have never seen it or any other 'unnatural' baits on this superb game-fishing river. The Annan seems so rich that the chub hardly need to eat bread, and it would almost certainly take time to educate them on to it.

Now to the old lady's cats, or *cat* as many people believe, amongst them the late Richard Walker, and Jim Gibbinson. In his book *Chub* (1975), Jim says, '. . . those Scottish cats must have pretty healthy appetites to demolish 10½lb of chub!' Richard Walker even went to the trouble of starving a cat for three days and then feeding it a chub of 3lb. The poor cat could not manage it! It was a shame really, because working from the wrong facts Walker wasted a good chub. In fairness to Jim, however, he did err on the side of Dr Cameron who, he noted, had no interest in the chub or the record, therefore refuting any suggestion of impropriety on the Doctor's part.

My conclusions, based on the above evidence, are that the Record Fish Committee were wrong to accept the chub in the first place only to reject it later, as they had undertaken absolutely no investigation whatsoever into the matter. It seems very odd to me that they rejected the fish through lack of proof, as they did not look for any in the first place. If they had taken this trouble, we would have a chub record of 10lb 8oz which would be virtually unbreakable, and unforgettable – instead of the present joke.

Thoughts and Recollections from the Annan

Fred Sykes

Living close to Carlisle, one would think that a desert of coarse fishing surrounds Fred Sykes, but the River Annan, just over the border into Scotland, draws him time and time again. Many words have been written about the fabled 'monsters' of the Annan, often by anglers who have made the occasional visit to the place, but here is a man who has really fished the river, specifically for chub, for years. His renowned tenacity has been rewarded with a breath-taking chub of no less than 6lb 5oz. What makes Fred's chapter so fascinating is that it contains the truth about the river. We are very privileged to have the chance to publish the details of his persistent campaign on the Annan, as opposed to the 'holiday trips' which form the basis of the majority of accounts to date about this particular river.

I shall never forget my first visit to Scotland's River Annan, some sixteen years ago now. Like so many English anglers before me I ventured across the border during the English close season; I was totally unprepared for the river that awaited me. The local bailiff pointed me in the direction of the nearest eight-pound chub swim and I duly set off with high hopes, bursting with excitement at the prospect of wetting a line in this most famous of chub rivers. Ten hours later, a very different angler made his weary way home, completely waterlicked and chubless!

Fortunately, I had spent the previous winter in the best-possible preparation for waterlicked anglers – a series of *Angling Times* Winter League matches held on the Yorkshire rivers; most of these were at Low Dunsforth, a hard nut to crack to say the least. These matches in Yorkshire taught me two great lessons: first, to work very hard on a swim; and second, *not* to miss the first bite when it eventually came! This was exceedingly important, because the second bite often never came! By applying these lessons on a return visit to the Annan, I captured my first-ever chub there, and shortly after that I caught my first four-pounder during a Chub Study Group get-together in the close season of 1973.

Those were early days for the Chub Study Group; and myself and my constant companion Slim Baxter drew great comfort from the fact that they, too, found the Annan a formidable proposition. One bite a day seemed the norm, which only underlined the importance of not missing that first bite.

The following year, the Carlisle Specimen Group was formed. Slim Baxter, Chris Bowman, Mike Noble and myself banded together, and one of our first projects was to catch a 5lb chub from one of the Solway rivers. After a period spent investigating condition factors and numerous scale readings, kindly done at the time by Dave Moore and Jim Gregory, we eventually concluded that the Annan seemed our best bet for a 5lb-plus chub. There was no evidence, however, of any monsters, but our findings suggested that a 21in chub from the Annan (measured from nose to fork of tail) might be one or two ounces heavier than comparable chub from the other Border rivers. At that time, our personal best fish were just falling short of 5lb, so one or two ounces would spell happiness!

And so began many trips over the Scottish border. I would hesitate to claim that any of us are 'Annan experts', but we probably have more first-hand experience of this challenging river than any other group of chub enthusiasts. However, this pseudo-scientific approach so beloved of specimen hunters soon made fools of us. There are so many other factors to be considered, and sure enough, our first 5lb chub came from the River Esk.

Back to the Annan, however. Our first trips were to the Royal Four Towns water, which in those days cost fifty pence a day, the ticket in fact a salmon and trout permit (in 1989, the cost was £5). Most first-time visitors to the Annan probably start on this stretch. If chub have a guardian angel, it is surely this piece of water.

A GAME RIVER

To the chub specialist who loves his intimate waters, with overhanging willows, beds of rushes and flood rafts, this stretch of the Annan comes as a shock. It is completely bereft of overhanging trees and bushes, and flows through open countryside. Some of the pools are enormous for what is, really, only a medium-sized river. There is no protection from the wind, and a slight breeze soon makes fishing difficult. Game anglers would describe it as sluggish and uninteresting, but when there is wind and rain about, as

138

High adventure into the unknown, in pursuit of monsters,
with Fred Sykes.

there often is in the far north-west of Britain, the Annan runs through like a train and the angler has difficulty standing up, let alone trying to fish. In those early days I used to feel like Captain Oates when I left the comfort of my car to lean into the wind and rain. High adventure into the unknown, in pursuit of monsters!

Fortunately, the rest of the Annan is not quite so featureless. The upper reaches are typical salmon and trout domains, with very few chub. The middle and lower stretches are much more interesting, with every kind of chub swim you could imagine. The only real difference to most other chub rivers is that everything is on a larger scale than the average angler expects. One feature that particularly excites me is the huge sandstone slabs that form some of the rocky pools, creating great ledges out in the river. Some of them have undercuts, both beneath the bank and in mid-river. Divers whom I once met on the river told me that some of these undercuts are enormous, forming underwater caverns where the fish can lie with rock above their heads, holding position in the current — even safer from the angler than sitting under an overhanging branch, don't you think?

There is no mistaking, however, that this is a great game river and subject to spates. The floods can be quite frightening to behold, but they clear quickly, and drop quite quickly, too. And the chub, when they are not in their obvious swims, are in salmon lies and the streamy water.

It is worth mentioning that the Annan is pretty well pollution-free, especially if you can turn a blind eye to the plastic bag or two floating by, and the odd bottle or beer can. Everybody dreams of the chance to fish in splendid surroundings for virgin fish, uneducated fish that bite freely, and the Annan fits the bill beautifully. It *ought* to be like taking candy from a baby, but it simply is not. I could name many very competent anglers who have gone home with their tail between their legs! I myself would top this list, as I have struggled on the river on quite a few occasions.

There are reasons for this difficulty — Annan chub are not quite as numerous as on other chub rivers. Most of the chub that fall to the game anglers meet with a somewhat predictable fate. This no longer upsets me as it once did, because I respect the game angler's right to manage his fishery as he thinks fit. I, too, have a fishery (containing carp) and make rules about stocking and culling, and I expect them to be obeyed. Removal of some fish leaves room for others to grow bigger. This may mean more blank sessions on the Annan for me, but that suits me fine in my pursuit of better than average chub. Surprisingly, the game anglers do not catch very many large chub, but they do catch quite a lot of small ones, especially when they are fishing small wet flies in the spring and early summer. From time to time I have seen distressing piles of 8 to 10in chub thrown up the bank; however, I have also met salmon anglers who have fished for years with worm and never seen a chub. Some regular visitors to the river did not even know the river held chub, despite the fact that their legered worms were in my favourite chub swims. Perhaps big chub rarely hook themselves; salmon certainly do! Nevertheless, I think there are more chub in the Annan than is generally supposed. Sticking my neck out, I would say that virgin chub are sometimes harder to catch than educated ones.

TACKLE AND BAIT

On tackle and bait, there are no tips I can give to the experienced chub angler. Chub are a most obliging fish, yet there are very few Annan chub that have been hooked once, let alone twice. Most will rarely see an angler's hook; no, tackle and bait is not the problem. Catching Annan chub is a matter of location, and not underestimating their finely tuned instinct for

There are swims which are, in fact, pools within pools.

'A certain flow, just off the pace.'

self-preservation. It might only be a simple matter of location, but location is not always that easy. Locating chub in small swims with obvious features is not difficult, but in some of the large Annan swims it is far from easy. Reading a river well is a skill – no, a gift – that few anglers possess. There are swims which are in fact 'pools within pools', and getting to know a river intimately can take years – perhaps more years than I have got!

I recently discovered Reg Righyni's book, *Salmon-Taking Times*, which contains a brilliant chapter on 'Reading River Currents'. This, and a pair of polaroid sunglasses, has opened up a whole new world to me. I have often thought that chub like, in Mr Righyni's words, 'a certain flow, just off the pace'. Righyni's book has made me think a lot more about it. It is really just as well that tackle and bait are not the problem, because in most parts of the river there is limited freedom of choice anyway. There are very few stretches where the chub angler can fish unhindered, and some where he cannot fish at all. Most owners and associations have very strict rules during the salmon and trout season, designed to protect the game fish and prevent poaching. Some of these rules make life difficult for the genuine chub angler. The more common restrictions include fly only, worm only in flood,

142

no legering, no maggots, no groundbaiting, no keepnets, no floats, etc., etc. Very few stretches allow any fishing at all in the short close season for game fish which runs from 16 November to 24 February, although this could be a prime time for chub. Basically I have to fish for chub with a salmon permit and salmon rules for 90 per cent of my time.

ANNAN MONSTERS

Well, what about the monsters in the river? I hope one day to meet Dr Cameron and talk to him about his remarkable chub. On the evidence to date I personally accept his fish – but what about the other reported, less publicised, monsters of the Annan?

Throughout my chubbing days I have come across a number of anglers with tales of monster chub. The largest of them was a fish which was claimed to be an incredible 14lb. And the man who told me of it looked me straight in the eye! Another game angler sent me off to a road-bridge 'where you can see them – into the tens of pounds.' My favourite quote is from a chap who professed, 'Never caught a big chub myself – but I've had them up to six and seven pounds on the fly.' Ten years later his comment still brings tears to my eyes.

Sorting out fact from fiction is virtually impossible. It seems that chub, above all other fish species, are the subject of extravagant claims; the first big chub an angler sees on the bank looks *huge*. Think back to the first chub you caught yourself. Three-pound chub often look four pounds to the beginner. I think it is something to do with the huge mouth a chub has in proportion to its body, together with its big, brassy scales. With the possible exception of carp, no other fish of any species sports such large scales for its size. Perhaps, big mouth + big scales = big chub fantasies?

However, a few years ago I was talking to some salmon netsmen who were certain they had caught chub in excess of eight pounds from time to time. The fish were never weighed, but these men were handling eight-, nine- and ten-pound salmon every day. And once, in their company, when a 4lb chub was caught and weighed, their initial estimate of that chub was nearer three pounds than four. From their description of the chub they caught I am satisfied they had caught some very big fish indeed!

And what of the monster chub on rod and line in recent times? When my friends and I first ventured on to the Annan, we were assured that there were numbers of fish in the six- to seven-pound class (source: Scottish Tourist Board, 1972). Confirming that has proved rather difficult. Mike Noble left

143

our little specimen group in 1975 and the remaining three of us put in a lot of time and effort, six years' worth in fact, before the Annan yielded its first five-pounder to us, a wonderful specimen of 5lb 7oz which fell to Chris Bowman in 1979. That fish, if not a real monster chub, was undoubtedly a whopper, and it remains Chris's largest chub to this day, even though he has an enviable list of five-pound chub to his credit.

My first five-pounder fell to me on the Annan in 1983, after a wait of ten years, but I am noted for doing things the hard way. Perhaps the nearest I will come to seeing or catching an Annan monster is the 6lb chub I caught in 1988. Fifteen years of searching and waiting was rewarded at last as that fish slipped into the net. I shall never forget the measuring and weighing ceremony, not least because at the first weighing I experienced great disappointment as the pointer inexplicably registered only 4lb 12oz! My 8lb Avons had never been pulled round so far, and it seemed an age before I spotted the figure '7' in the little window. For the record, the chub measured 22½in from nose to fork, with a 15in girth, and weighed 6lb 5oz. Surely a semi-monster!

Sid Boulter, a very good friend, who travelled a 110-mile round-trip to witness and photograph that chub, has made two interesting comments that are worthy of repetition here. After returning the chub, we stood and watched in the torch beam as it swam out into mid-river. It looked massive! Sid turned to me and said, 'Fred, if a salmon angler saw that I'm sure he would estimate it at 8lb, maybe more.'

Later, when Sid heard I was contributing a chapter to this book, he asked, 'Are you going to say how hard it is? On second thoughts,' he said, 'the Annan isn't hard, it's a grueller.'

Of course, Sid's comments and most of my experience relates to winter fishing. In summer I am sure it's much kinder, and the chub may well be more obliging. The few summer chub I have caught have not been in good condition, so most of my chubbing is a winter pursuit.

Sitting at my window as I write, I can gaze across the Solway plain, over the Solway Firth to the four towers of the Chapelcross Power Station, situated behind Annan town. As the crow flies, it is about thirteen miles. By car it is about fifty miles, and sometimes an hour and a half away. I often look up and wonder if there are any monsters waiting for me over there. Presumably there are bigger chub than mine, somewhere in its forty miles or so. There is still that little bit of schoolboy magic in the Annan for me, the thrill of exploration of the unknown. So much of the Annan will never see a chub angler, and with all the restrictions the odds are in the fish's favour. In the future, the amount of available water is likely to decrease rather than increase as Timeshare and other schemes exclude the casual angler. Perhaps the Annan will always keep its secrets, but to me that is the essence of the place, and that is the challenge.

What Makes a Good Chub River?

Richard Smith

A non-angler, Richard is currently working on a thesis concerned with River Wensum chub and their habitat. It is most generous of Richard to take time off from his rather intensive project in order to contribute to this book, and for this we are grateful. He is sponsored by the Anglian Water Authority and we await the end result with considerable interest. Richard's contribution to this book is fascinating in itself. Written in layman's terms it cannot but help the chub angler's understanding of chub habitat and, in turn, of his own fishing. Neither of us have met a man more enthusiastic about chub than Richard, which says a lot considering he has never caught one on rod and line!

Richard has in the past undertaken a lot of work in determining the source of the terrible pollution problems on the River Waveney. He eventually traced it back to the intensive pig farming community in the Horham/Hoxne/Stradbroke area; whether the Anglian Water Authority actually stop the pollution is another matter. We pray for the day when somebody of Richard's sensitivity, understanding and drive is in a position to help the East Anglian rivers back to their rightful state of purity and cleanliness.

During a three-year Ph.D. study, sponsored by Anglian Water, my interest has been on chub and river habitat. I have been trying to discover some of the river features that chub prefer, in order to help fisheries management.

Every chub angler knows that if there is an overhanging tree by the river, there may be a chub beneath it. This is particularly the case when the branches are actually submerged in the water. Although I am not an angler, I have spent many hours dangling over the river in a tree, watching the chub beneath; but the most exciting views are from within the river while snorkelling, since chub can be seen lurking in the crevices created by the algae-coated branches.

Chub-land!

I suppose a major task in my work has been to determine the numbers of chub in the rivers of Norfolk and Suffolk in order that I can relate these to habitat. Electric fishing is an accurate way to catch most chub in a river, and to help me with this technique Anglian Water provide the equipment and expertise. We stretch large stop-nets across the river 200 yards apart, to enclose all the fish, and then using ropes from each bank we pull a boat upstream, zig-zagging all the way so that most of the river can be sampled. Two people in the boat stun the fish with electric anodes, and as the fish float to the surface they are easily caught in hand-nets. At the end of the day we count all the fish, weigh them, measure their length and give them a tattoo characteristic for each site.

Some anglers have expressed concern about this electric fishing, and wonder whether fish are damaged. I must admit, I have had my worries on some occasions but I think if the gear is used properly there is no problem. I have recaptured many of the same chub (some up to five times, recognised by their tattoo), and their condition is comparable to those that have been electro-fished for the first time.

As many anglers already know, the river Wensum is an ideal river to learn about chub and habitat. It hasn't always had plenty of chub, but was stocked by the River Board[1] with approximately 1,080 fish between 1955 and 1965. Different batches of 100 to 300 individuals were taken from the River Wye, and some from the River Colne (a tributary of the Thames), and gradually stocked into the river. The River Wensum, for those who think it is just a myth, really is a clear-running river, and is of course famous for its large fish. The crystal-clear waters are in summer capable of producing some superb, pristine-looking, well-proportioned fish. Chub are no exception; in fact all the fish we catch are like jewels – including chub, dace and roach.

As you might expect, most chub have been caught from typical swims. Trees are a classic feature, as are undercut banks and floating marginal reeds. Without doubt, the most exciting reaches are downstream of water-mills where tens of chub are often caught; 5lb 6oz is the largest so far. In these stretches dace are also common and are solid-looking fish of between 6 and 9oz. Every now and again the odd roach turns up, and is invariably over 1lb, sometimes over 2lb. The Wensum's barbel are enormous (10lb or more), and even the ruffe and gudgeon are large.

Most of the chub do not seem to move great distances, although some with tattoos have been recaptured a few miles from their original site. Two were even caught by anglers in Lyng Eastaugh gravel pit. I imagine they managed to swim into these river-valley pits during a heavy flood, since a local eel fisherman accidentally caught many tattooed chub in his fyke-nets set on the meadows (of all places!) whilst fishing for eels. During the winter, nearly all of the smaller chub disappeared from the river, and naturally I was puzzled. Perhaps they had been washed downstream. However, I managed to find one very large mixed shoal of marked dace and small chub in a small, secluded mill-pool next to the main river. They had moved upstream to overwinter away from the main flow and could be recognised by their tattoos. The following summer they returned to the main river; some of the same dace even returned to their exact positions, 2 miles downstream.

HABITAT

So what are the habitat features that make the ideal chub river? A chub prefers 'those streams in which the water flows with some considerable rapidity, along a clean bottom of sand or gravel; and so needful to its well-

'Those streams in which the water flows with some rapidity.'

being is a supply of what is afforded by current, that it is not easy to keep it alive in a tank, or within the narrow limits of a pond.' This was written in 1862 by Couch,[2] and my thoughts are exactly the same. Adult chub show a marked preference for flowing water, and although they can survive in still water (some of the largest predatory chub are to be found in these areas), they are not numerous. Upstream of a water-mill in the more sluggish flow, there may be one or two chub under a tree, but in the stronger fast flow downstream of the mill, there could be ten to twenty chub under a very similar tree.

This pattern is repeated with such remarkable consistency in the River Wensum that it is actually possible to estimate from habitat data how many chub there will be in an unknown stretch of river. From the graph in the figure below I have been able to predict low numbers of chub in the River Bure, in Norfolk, because the river is slow. Chub numbers from the River Gipping in Suffolk were also accurately estimated in both the suitable and unsuitable reaches of the river. To predict the *correct number* of chub with reasonable accuracy, from habitat data, was quite unexpected. Normally we would expect any number of chub for a given amount of habitat, depending upon a whole range of factors such as

149

successful spawning, survival of young fish, degree of pollution, preda-
tion, etc. This was not the case, since we could estimate the numbers of
chub from flow data alone. I suspect that in the slow-flowing stretches
there is simply not enough drifting food to support many chub. Flow may
actually limit chub numbers – rivers which are slow do not have many
chub even after successful spawning.

If this argument is correct, then by creating a fast flow in a sluggish river
such as the Bure, we should eventually find more chub. To me this is a
crucial question, because we can now be optimistic and set out to rehabili-
tate some of the slow-flowing, silty rivers that are too wide and have a
gradient that is too gentle for the volume of water. At present, they provide
poor habitat because they are over-widened by the dredger or are ponded
by water-mills.

SPAWNING

Naturally, before all the suitable habitat becomes filled with adult chub,
there must be successful spawning and a good survival of young fish. Chub
are gravel spawners, and again seem to prefer the fast-flowing reaches.
Their eggs are sticky and easily suffocated by fine silt, so perhaps chub
choose a fast flow for spawning because of the clean gravel. When the fry
hatch they seem to spend most of their time in shallow, slow-flowing areas
of rivers. In the larger rivers, very shallow margins such as drinking places
for cattle, which receive plenty of sunshine, are favourite places for chub
fry. Small rivers such as the River Tud, a tributary of the Wensum, are also
excellent nursery areas since these are often shallow and have many areas of
moderate flow over clean gravel. Chub fry pick at the food in amongst this
gravel and seem to be dependent on river temperature. In fact other
research[3] has clearly shown that warm summers aid the survival of chub fry.
Although the reasons are not fully understood, perhaps a good growth of
fry in warm years helps them to pass rapidly through a delicate stage of their
lives. After a few summers, chub gradually move into deeper water, first
into the fast runs where they mix with dace, and later to the classic chub
swims such as those beneath bankside cover.

It is not uncommon to find chub populations dominated by fish of one
age, because the survival of fry in some years is poor. This seems to be the
case on the River Wensum in the stretch downstream of Costessey Mill.
During electro-fishing we caught seventy-five chub in half a mile of the river,
and only two of these were less than 12in long. Most were large fish born in

Tony Miles with 5lb 7oz of Wensum chub.

the 1970s. Survival of young fish in these years must have been particularly good, and perhaps due to the very warm summers of 1975 and 1976. Unless these chub are replaced by younger fish from other unknown parts of this stretch, numbers must soon naturally fall as these fish die (some of them are now 13 to 14 years old). Indeed, some anglers have expressed their fears; Tony Miles, in his book on chub, mentions that 'the numbers are steadily declining . . . something is seriously wrong, that is for certain.' I would like to refer him to the case during the 1960s in the River Stour, Dorset. Anglers complained that specimen chub had disappeared but research by Richard Mann[4] indicated that this would only be temporary. He was proved right. The survival of chub fry was predicted to be particularly successful during the warm summer of 1959, and as these fish grew, by the late 1960s good fishing was once again restored.

It therefore seems that in some rivers there is a natural cycle in chub numbers due to the weather. If numbers do fall at Costessey, let us hope it is similar to the Dorset Stour in the 1960s and that they bounce back after the next good year of recruitment. The future for chub populations in other parts of the Wensum looks more certain, as small fish are more numerous. Downstream of Taverham Mill is a good example; I have caught and seen fish of all ages in the small side-channels and cattle-drinks.

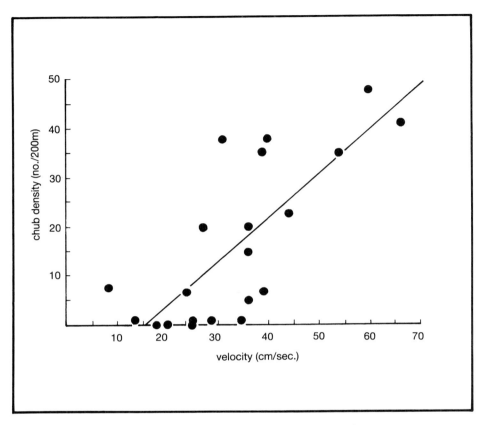

A graph illustrating the relationship between the number of chub and the average river speed at twenty-one sites on the River Wensum. (Each point represents one site which is 200m long. Those sites with a fast flow have more chub.)

If I were asked to pick ideal chub conditions, I would choose a healthy-looking river with a fast flow over clean gravel. There must be plenty of cover and sheltered areas where chub can rest. Chub fry should be a common sight, so the river must have plenty of nursery areas, such as large, shallow bays or even small, gentle-flowing tributaries nearby. Interestingly, these are probably the natural features of fairly warm, fast-flowing rivers. They have not been over-dredged, so they flow in steep-sided canyons and have little fry habitat; every obstacle in the river has not been removed, so chub have somewhere to rest, and they have not been ponded by water-mills, so most of the river is fast flowing with plenty of drifting food.

NOTES

1. East Suffolk and Norfolk River Board, *Annual Reports* 1953–65.
2. Couch, *Fishes of the British Isles*, 4 vols. 8vo., 1862–65.
3. Mann, R.H.K. (1976). 'Observations of the age, growth, reproduction and food of the chub *Squalis cephalus* (L.) in the River Stour, Dorset', *Journal of Fish Biology*, vol. 8: pp. 265–88.
4. *Ibid.*

Days with Dace

John Bailey and Roger Miller

Obviously, if you have bought this book then you are a serious angler, but even so it can be possible sometimes to confuse a very large dace with a very small chub! It has certainly happened to us in the past with those occasional super 'double figure' dace – that is, a fish of over 10oz in weight. Dace like this can be a bit confusing. They have developed a thickness in the body that is not typically streamlined and dace-like. The shoulders have become bullish and the head large. Above all, the mouth no longer has that fine delicacy usually associated with a 4oz or 6oz fish. Even the colours of the flanks and the back can deepen to become more the bronze of the chub and less the silver and dark green of the typical dace. It pays, therefore, to carry out the basic tests on a really big dace – for, as Fred J. Taylor once remarked, we 'can spend our lives trying to catch a pounder and when we do it will be a little chub!' To unravel the vital differences between chub and dace, the most obvious point of distinction to begin with is the anal fin, and we make no apology for stating what has already been stated many times in the past – that the anal fin of the chub is convex (curved outwards), and that of the dace is concave (curved inwards). Although the head of the chub is far more rounded than that of the dace, especially when they are lying side by side, the acid test is the anal fin.

The poor dace! For so long their best use was seen as livebaits for pike (a disgusting practice if ever there was one), both in East Anglia and in far-flung waters. God only knows how many of these silver darts have been harvested from the clear streams of East Anglia only to end up on the end of a treble hook in the Fens or on the Broads. The River Yare at Bawburgh, Marlingford and Barford was completely denuded of its dace stocks as greedy pike men poured them into giant tubs and drove them up the motorways to Loch Lomond in the 1970s. The Yare dace have never recovered, and neither have the dace at that one-time dace stretch *par excellence* – the River Wensum at Attlebridge. Obviously dace do not inspire the passion that chub can and do, but we have always found them to be well worth the catching. Smaller dace are quick, clean, obliging and make a winter's day long-trotting a lovely experience. Bigger fish, however, the 'doubles', present a true specialist challenge. The true pounder is a target probably as difficult as a chub six times that weight.

Though chub have adapted well to still waters, dace almost invariably do not. They will live in lakes, but they rarely do well there, and remain small and generally anaemic. Give them a current, however, and the dace are totally in their element. The river need not be large: Norfolk's River Tud, for example, is the tiniest of streams but the dace come out as big as a pound most seasons. This is reflected elsewhere, and small rivers such as the Lark and the Thet consistently produce excellent fish to the few that know those rivers intimately. At the other end of the scale, dace thrive equally as well in the very largest of rivers, and some of our earliest very large dace were taken from that massive, border river the Tweed, and in Ireland from the Cork Blackwater. In Wales, the great, rolling Wye holds potentially record dace, and down in the south of England the chalk streams and rivers have always been prolific. Nowhere, though, are dace rivers more beautiful than in the north of England; the Ure, Nidd, Dane and the Cumberland Eden are all delights for the keen 'dacer' where the quick, clear waters seem to reflect the very nature of the species itself.

The dace season is a very long one. The extreme heat of high summer does not worry the fish, and in the direst of winter months we have found them to be the ones most willing to feed when temperatures plummet well below freezing point. They will feed all day long, and as dusk descends dace will feed harder still. In truth, at any time of the day, be it in bright sunlight or dull and overcast, in arctic or tropical conditions, dace will mouth a bait as long as it is presented correctly. Low, clear water does not put them down and thickly coloured floodwater will not dampen their willingness to oblige, once you find them. If we do have a favourite period of our own, then it is probably during the last days of the season when the weather is mild once more and the dace are highly active. They are also heavier. Spawning takes place in the early spring, and in March many of them are truly 'pigeon-chested'. This is undoubtedly *the* fortnight when the chance of a 1lb dace is a real and genuine possibility.

DACE SWIMS

Dace swims are highly varied but we will say that in our experience the shallow, rapid, streamy stretches of river hold the greater number of smaller fish. Of course, 'doubles' do sometimes turn up here on very light tackle, but this is an exception and not a rule. No, the larger dace tend to be in other areas. On the Norfolk rivers we have found the best big dace swims to be the weir and mill-pools, the slower stretches above the mills, the deep bends and slacks, eddies behind fallen trees or other obstructions, feeder con-fluences, long, deep, steady runs and finally any deep, reasonably well-scoured ox-bows. Of course, it could easily be said that we have just described the archetypal big roach and chub swims. That is exactly it! This is how we have caught our big dace, for as big fish I see them as having similar requirements to the other larger species that I also pursue.

Our observations on the Norfolk rivers are also applicable to much larger rivers, such as the Tweed, Wye or Blackwater. There, dace have fallen to us as we have roach fished the great slacks and eddies dozens of yards across, or in the deep, slow pools, or behind bridge piles, or even in the murky water beside the once-infamous bacon factory at Cappoquin in Ireland. The message appears to be that for big dace, the spacious swims are a favourite.

EQUIPMENT AND TACTICS

Trotting the stream is fun, and should always be that. A small stick float with a no. 6 or 8 shot placed at intervals down the line, a 1.7lb test bottom to a size 18 hook with a single or double maggot or caster, constitutes a favourite rig. Sometimes the bites are very quick or do not even register. In this case, the 'tell-tale' shot, usually a no 8 (dust), is in the wrong position. About eighteen inches up from the hook is generally the most telling place to start, but move it down to about a foot if problems continue. Loose feed is often quite enough to keep the dace interested, but sometimes bait mixed into groundbait, and mixed hard, can pull them down to the bottom where bites seem generally easier to hit. Feed can be overdone, however – shoal dace are not large and their appetites are limited. Six, seven or eight maggots each swim down is the average on the more modest rivers. Naturally, it is advisable substantially to increase the amount of loose feed you introduce when fishing the larger-scale rivers we have mentioned. It is also tempting to throw in a handful of maggots before the start, but this has in the past killed a swim stone dead. Little and often is our dace way now, gradually building a swim up to a climax.

The big dace in the deeper, slower waters are a completely different fish. For them, maggots are no longer our favourite bait and we now use flake almost exlcusively. In many ways this is roach fishing dramatically scaled down. The line can be 2 to 3lb, but the hook should only be a 12 or 14, covered by just a pinch of bread. The weight should be as light as possible with bite indication super-sensitive, in order to cope with the dace's lightning power of rejection. A very delicate quivertip is the usual tool, but if the current is slow enough then we find a butt indicator will give a bit more time to strike. There are times when big dace fairly bang into a bait and hook themselves, however clumsy the presentation, but these fish are rare in the extreme. We always set out to fish as neatly and as tightly as is humanly possible. Feeding again has to be light. Even a 12oz dace is not a truly big fish and can so easily be overfed. Half a slice of mashed bread is a good start, and a further quarter of a slice can be fed in each cast. We try to keep the baiting and the casting as accurate as possible with these small amounts, because the bread can swirl around the pool and be easily lost, doing little or no good.

For the very best of the big dace, we invariably stay on up to a couple of hours into darkness. Whilst smaller dace will feed happily in daylight, there are those exceptional fish that have drifted into near-nocturnal habits, and it is no surprise to us that most of our big dace photographs are taken by flash in very low light conditions.

DACE ON THE FLY

We do not feel we can end this chapter without a mention of fly fishing for dace. Never for a moment would we say that artificials are as effective for dace – or for chub – as a real bait, but the method is a delight in itself. Many times during an evening, dace will come up to dimple the surface as they sip in hatching flies, and a dry fly can then take them in the purest of ways. We have not found dace to be over-critical of the fly patterns and any small (say, size 18) black, blue or white pattern will attract them. There does not seem to be quite the need to match the hatches as there is with trout or even grayling, but good presentation, as in all dace fishing, is vitally important. If the fly is presented over the fish with the least amount of drag upon it, it will be refused. At the best of times the take is a very rapid one and the strike has to be immediate and firm. However, we must confess that our striking success rate is rarely better than one in three chances, and it is frequently more like one in six! Still, a dace safely risen, hooked and landed on the fly is a capture to be treasured, and the whole delicacy of the art is exquisite.

There are millions of dace throughout Britain, so it would be idle to suggest their presence is threatened in a serious way. There is no doubt, however, that their numbers are in decline for several reasons. Abstraction, pollution, livebait removal and chemical infiltration all play their deadly part. Equally, if not more dangerous, is the dredging and canalising of rivers that has taken place all over England since the 1960s. Dace need currents and streamy gravels very much indeed, but a straight, uniform drain of a river that runs like a train after winter rains does nothing for the fry and yearlings that find it virtually impossible to maintain their position without shelter.

In north Norfolk, the upper River Bure once held great dace stocks until the river was 'improved' in the 1960s. Thereafter, numbers fell steadily until in certain stretches, populations were virtually non-existent. This was the case at Abbot's Hall, until eight or nine years ago when a trout syndicate stepped in. Numerous groynes were built to scour the mud and clean the gravels. These groynes also gave shelter to small fish, and it was soon discovered that dace were beginning to return to the stretch for the first time since the Anglian Water Authority had stepped in. Today, the stretch is once again very rich in dace, and when electro-fished in the winter, dace are *always* found behind the groynes. This one physical improvement has radically altered the river, again making it suitable for dace, by creating the habitat which they need in order to survive.

The lesson here is real and obvious, and we deeply hope that coarse anglers and their clubs will soon show the same concern for real river improvements as the Abbot's Hall syndicate has done. Every club secretary knows the problems of getting the members out in working parties, but it must be done if river fish are to be safeguarded. We are charged with the most important of duties as we move into the twenty-first century and the dace, as one of our most vulnerable of river species, demands immediate concern.

Index